SEAN PURDY

Rescue Dog To Super Dog

The ultimate rescue dog training guide: discover how to
transform your anxious rescue dog into a problem free,
obedient to–be, loyal friend for life

First edition published 2020
© Sean Purdy

Contents

Rescue Dog To Super Dog

JUST A LITTLE SOMETHING FROM THE AUTHOR, AND A SPECIAL BOOK BUYERS BONUS

To my Rescue dog owners,

Thank you for buying my book, this will be a life changing experience for you and your dog.

As a bonus for your commitment and dedication for your dog, I want to gift to you a free digital version of this book so you can read it on your phone or tablet whenever you want to.

To get access right now to this valuable resource go to:

www.onedogtraining.co.uk/resources/free-stuff

Until next time

Sean Purdy
Rescue Dog Whisperer
www. onedogtraining.co.uk

Consistency and Calm

This book is for all those rescue dog owners, and owners of problematic dogs, who want to give a dog a second chance instead of giving up on that dog. You're my inspiration for writing this book and I plan on helping each and everyone of you to understand your dog, train your dog and have that dog for the rest of their life.

Introduction

WHY YOU NEED THIS BOOK

In my experience there are a fair few dog trainers who promote multiple training methods to help the owners succeed with their dog's unacceptable behavior, especially with rescue dogs. Unfortunately, these shitty methods rarely work (Yes! I just said shitty), because most dog trainers apply training concepts to dogs that have behavioral issues.

Big no no!

Now the problem is dog trainers should be used for clients that have relatively balanced dogs that are good most of the time but just don't have general obedience training, or maybe they lack discipline. So basically 90% of the time, this wouldn't be a rescue dog and that's when you have the behavioral issues.

A trainer then should not try to work on a dog displaying any behavioral issues like Aggression, Separation Anxiety, High Dominance, Resource Guarding, Hyper Sensitivity and excitement and so on and so on!

Again, big no no!

Dog training can look to be an easy thing; simple some would say. The thing is a lot of dogs I train have behavioral issues that you might have with *your* dog. With behavioral issues, a standard dog training routine is just not going to cut it.

These are the routines that should be used on dogs that are already controllable and can be tamed easily.

You may notice when trying to give your dog a command that they pull a deaf one: they pretend they haven't heard you (They have heard you) Then I come in and that dog listens, maybe not straight away but it's because of a poor leadership relationship between you and your dog, or your dog feeling insecure, or possibly not fully trusting humans because of past issues or dominance issues. Listening to you right now is not at the top of their priority, I'm afraid.

So what do you do?

You get in a behaviorist like *cough, cough* Sean Purdy – The Rescue Dog Whisperer.

OR

You read the rest of this book and stay consistent and

follow my training to a tee, and you will have a much happier, calm and attentive dog that waits on your beckoning call and directive.

I mean you've bought my book for a reason, but don't take my word for it, please read all the positive testimonials on my site or on Google and you'll find out I get the positive results you and your dog need.

How to use this book

Ok so this book is not the longest, and it's not meant to be, I've tried to get all my knowledge and dog training gems in this book without the fluff and crap that most dog books leave you with.

Please use this book as a guide to lead you through the path of training your dog the **right way** - the rescue dog way. Please read from start to finish. Yes, in that order. Practice what I preach. Be consistent. Have fun. Then when you get to chapter 6 **Time to Get Practical,** you'll have the chance to find the main training issues you're having and then you can follow the exercises I have given right flat bang in that section.

Once you have read it through, then jump to the section that applies the most to you and your dog. Please re-read the chapter regarding dog behavior as this is where the most bang for the buck comes in to play. I would even say if there's only one bit you read then let it be that part.

I'll also be interchanging between him and her when referring to a dog.

If you follow the above, you will not go wrong.

I will point out its consistency on your part to follow and put the training into place, I can only tell you and hold your hand through this book. The thing is, that's as far as I go. It's then up to you to be consistent.

It rings true, especially for rescue dogs; they need consistency; they need a direction to follow, and they need a calm and consistent leader.

I train you the owner to train your dog.

Oh, and yes, you will hear the word C.O.N.S.I.S.T.E.N.C.Y A lot in this book.

Ok, so without further ado… Let's get to it.

CHAPTER 1

HOME BOUND, WHAT NOW?

I remember when we first had Atty; he came 7 weeks early. We were not prepared one bit, our lives got flipped around and so did poor Lilla's (my dog) I knew it would be a testing time ahead, lot's of learning, lot's of pooey nappies and no sleep. Apart from the pooey nappies, bringing a dog home for the first time can have similar experiences.

The first few weeks will be the testing times; it's usually in these first 2 weeks where around 20% of rescue dogs get sent back to the rescue shelter. This is where the mistakes happen because of pre-conceived ideas the owner had about what they thought they needed to do. How can it go from happy to crappy in such a brief time?

We take our rescue doggies to their forever home, driving off into the sunset ready to give them all the things they never had, and because we're human, we like to humanise things, and it's in the next couple of weeks - what we do as owners - that will determine the fate of our new dog.

Mistake #1—*My dog needs the comfort of a sofa or my bed, to feel safe and welcome. Right?*

Wrong! The last thing your new rescue dog needs is a dozen different options of furniture choices. They've not been living their days dreaming of their future owners letting them do what they want! All they want is a calm leader. What starts out as self-inviting themselves onto your furniture or bed, then moves on to behavioural problems like jumping up, barking, rushing through doorways before you, being food possessive, resource guarding over their perceived valuable areas… Your bed.

Now the thing is you probably already know some history about your dog, but you still yet don't know your dog's correct behaviour and tendencies.

Mistake #2—*My dog needs freedom, full reign of the house from being confined in that shelter, right?*

Again, No sorry! What your dog needs now more than ever is rules and a calm and consistent leader. Too much freedom and full run of the house can become overwhelming, and what happens when a dog gets overwhelmed in a strange place? They go wee wee. Now dogs do this for many reasons: anxiety; scent marking their unfamiliar territory or scared and unsure of what to do.

Well my friend, this is where you, as a calm and confident leader, come in. Don't worry if you don't feel like one, because by the end of this book, you'll be your dogs' superhero. You need to set up the environment for your dog to be trouble-free, so don't give your dog the chance to misbehave or be destructive, so move anything valuable you don't want chewed, like? sofa arm chairs: this is where you set a boundary.

So what you want to do is set up their area, ideally in the kitchen, with a crate and bed ready for them and a doggie gate on the doorway to create those boundaries for the first couple of weeks. This will help your dog to settle in. Remember, we need to establish rules and boundaries; as a dog's natural state is calmness when they have a job and direction coming from a calm and confident leader. This way you're ruling out the option of any reason for your dog to get in to any trouble. Leave everything your dog may need, so a fresh bowl of water/a filled Kong for distraction.

When you first bring your dog home, let them outside or give them the option to go in the garden straight away to sniff around and toilet if needed.

Establish these rules for the first few weeks, remember

you don't want your dog to have free roam of the house. I know this might go against the belief of some so-called trainers who would give a free rein of the house only to then find later a plethora of behavioural problems that stem from no boundaries.

When you feel it is ready, then you can let your dog have free roam of your house: you'll learn more as we go through the book together.

Mistake #3–*Not giving your dog a consistent daily exercise routine.*

They need mental stimulation as much as physical exercise, as it is what tires and entertains your dog (I include significant exercise games to tire and entertain in Chapter 8) Exercise along with mental stimulation encourages a calm dog. Too much pent-up energy from under exercise will lead to destructive behaviour.

Now I'm not saying you have to take your dog on many walks or even a walk a day (As I write this, we're in lockdown–self isolation) Just create plenty of opportunities for your dog to tire themselves out, or mentally stimulate themselves. Start by just following these books' principles and the training psychology will mentally stimulate your dog and tire them out. Then you can introduce snuffle mats and Don't know what these are? Don't worry, I go over these in Chapter 8.

When you take your dog out, introduce her to a 10 metre horse lunge lead; these are ideal for letting them think they're off lead. They can run around and burn some energy and you can practice recall safely, where you know your dog will not run away. You can play fetch, throw her treats and practice attentiveness exercises.

Do not use this for the first couple weeks, your rescue dog needs to first get used to her new surroundings and secondly behave on a short leash first.

Mistake #4—*My dog can have whatever she wants, she's had a hard life. Right?*

If you want a well behaved, non-resource guarding dog, then I recommend not showering your dog with every toy your nearest pet shop has to offer. Buy a few different toys and rotate them, don't just give your dog free range to all the toys whenever she wants... This is a recipe for resource guarding and this can lead to aggression and you could get bitten. Now you don't want that, trust me it hurts!

Giving them ALL toys is not the way to their heart, leadership and direction are along with the gospel CONSISTENCY. If you let your dog turn in to a diva, she'll act that way and before long, she'll get territorial over the sofa.

So what do you do?

You start the play and you finish the play, when you want the play to end, you should be able to get the toy. I recommend using the "leave it command" and also rotate toys, make it a game to find your dogs most valued toy and then find 2nd best and 3rd best toys, use this to get control of your dog, doing so will help longer term when you want their attention on walks, as long as you have created the leadership in-house.

Mistake #5—*My dog had a horrible life previously, so now needs me to shower him with affection in the form of cuddles, kisses… Oh and being allowed on the sofa bed and feeding from hand. Right?*

As owners we allow our dogs to invade our personal space, jumping up on the sofa, sleeping on our beds, but then when we get up to make a drink and almost trip up over our dog because they've become so attached to us, we get angry and tell them off.

Dogs need consistency, not mixed signals and confusion with the rules. If we mollycoddle them, they soon get attached to us under the pretense of insecurity and this can lead to a feeling of possession of us where they'll get aggressive when another dog or human comes up to us.

That's a big no no. You do not want it to get to that point.

You need to follow the above rules in the mistakes, allow your dog to have their own space, rules to follow, and consistent leadership for a well-balanced rescue dog, especially in the first few weeks of bringing your dog back into your home.

If you've just got a new dog, I can't stress enough why you need to follow these rules. Don't worry though as I go through all of this and more in the chapter to follow, so by the time you have finished this book as long as you follow it and are consistent, you'll have a happy content and calm rescue dog, that will be in their forever home.

The first couple of days and weeks

- Give your dog time to acclimatise to their new surroundings. Don't invite every Tom, Dick and Harry over to see your dog. Also, let them get used to you and any other pack members first, so if you have children, tell them how they need to behave around their new dog. No rushing up and overwhelming him.

- For the first few days follow the feeding schedule and diet that the rescue centre advised. This is to avoid any sloppy messes on the floor first thing in the morning when you wake up… Yes Lilla my dog, the One Dog Training mascot did this at some point, well a few times actually.

- Don't let your dog off lead until you know they trust you and definitely not until you have great recall. Also, don't bring them to the park for the first few days, get used to walking around your streets and nailing walking to heel.

- Help at night—Your rescue dog might have separation anxieties; this will be worse if you ignore all above and don't give your dog rules or boundaries and don't show any sign of a calm and confident leader. What you need to do is develop independence in your dog. If your dog whines at night, you need to vocally correct that behaviour, and show them they have their crate: their safe place. Start as you mean to go on, be consistent, don't give in, and within a few days your dog will be used to sleeping downstairs in a crate or bed by themselves.

CHAPTER 2

THE RESCUED AND THE RESCUER

Before I tell you the mind-set of a rescue, I want to start with a brief story. The story of Lilla - the rescue puppy.

It all started with her carefree, easy mum formerly known as Narla looking for some quick action on a summer's evening. Well she got just that after escaping her garden. Her then owners couldn't cope when they found out she was pregnant, so she ended up at the wonderful rescue center Just For Dogs.

Well, my partner Tania was strolling through her Facebook feed and stumbled upon a post from Just For Dogs, who were looking to re-home mum and her 10 puppies. I want to tell you now: We were not looking for a puppy. We wanted Narla; we came to visit her; she was beautifully calm with a submissive side to her but for us this was not meant to be as she already had someone waiting to re-home her.

So, we had a look at the remaining three puppies, one girl

and two boys. We chose the crazy girl, not realizing at the time the pain in the arse she would end up being, (she's an exceptional dog but hard work, keep reading and you'll find out why).

Our world was about to be turned upside down.

Fast forward a few months we had a cute bundle of craziness and we did what most owners do, we went online and typed in "How to train a puppy" and clicked on the first thing that came up, then we did that another two times and got tips and advice from the online dog training "gurus" promising this and that. It went great for a brief time, then she showed signs of her personality type: she had hit her adolescent stage.

To make it even worse, Atticus our son came 7 weeks early, and the training went out of the window. I got back from the hospital elated and shattered and came into a home with pieces of ripped up lino; the same lino we had installed the week before. In the next 3 months things got gradually worse, she started toileting in the house, whining and howling at night, she was barking back at us, jumping up at us and anyone who came into the house, she pulled like a train on a walk and it was that bad she broke Tania's finger when on a walk; She showed signs of aggression towards other dogs and was displaying all passive dominant traits

(You'll learn those traits later in the book).

As owners, she broke us, wore us down, and we had two options left. **Re-home her or get a behaviorist in.** Thankfully, even though in our extremely sleep deprived state, we still loved her and got in a behaviorist that was recommended to us. We were taught the right way to train, talk and listen to a dog and by the end of the first session we had seen a change in Lilla, a light at the end of the tunnel, she could be a well-behaved dog.

After this profound experience I had, it ignited a passion in me I didn't know I wanted until then, and spurred me on to train many more dogs. I created One Dog Training, training dogs in person and online, creating a thriving online community and would be known as the Rescue Dog Whisperer. I have worked with many more dogs and owners of rescue dogs, help them understand their dog and how to train them and gain back that control and be that calm leader a dog needs.

Now I want you to know a few stats, I could've fallen into one of these if I didn't get a behaviorist in. I Talked with two rescue centers and one told me from Jan 2019–April 2020 out of 140 dogs re-homed 11 were returned, these are good stats and that rescue center adopted the approach of only giving a suitable dog to a suitable family. The issues for returning the dog was because of the owner's unwillingness to work with the dog and not understanding why the dog was doing what they were doing, a breakup in a relationship and finally an owner illness or death.

Understanding a rescue

Rescue dogs arrive at a rescue shelter for many reasons. They could have been previously abused, neglected or abandoned, usually left on the streets and saved from euthanasia. However, more dogs go to rescue centers because the owner doesn't know how to control the dog. Just think about that for a while. Often the rescue centers know little at all about the dog's previous life's before being rescued. Dogs arrive with tales to tell but rarely people know how to listen to what're saying, it's only the really committed and caring of rescue centers, through experience, that work on understanding those dogs tales and listen to them (Not these crappy rescues just in it for the money and will re home to anyone).

It's also the skill of behaviorists to be able to understand a dog, to be able to listen to the dogs' needs; their behavior's and why they do what they do, and then to be able to transfer said skills to YOU the owner so they (you) can better understand your dog and be able to give the necessary and correct training.

Now with your normal non-rescued dog this is a lot easier, but with rescues they may not know how to be around humans, they might feel scared, anxious, aggressive, they might have been previously abused and in those cases may not even attack, they'll just go in on themselves.

It's sad it's like their fight-or-flight response is broke and they just give up on life.

This makes helping you train your rescue dog that much sweeter, the positive results and behavioral changes I get. The look on a clients face when they see their dog respond positively, differently than they've seen before or the look of the rescue dog when he sees' a calm leader that he can trust and follow.

A rescue dog needs that little extra bit of commitment, safety, and consistency.

Recently I had a pair of rescue dogs called Butters and Blossom, not much information known regarding their past lives as strays, but I realized both of them were not used to a lead and collar. The sight of a collar made them back away, let alone showing them a lead. The first session was just getting them used to a collar and then slight tension and release on a lead.

The thing with dogs is as soon as you show consistency calmly and follow through, they quickly change perception of what to like and not like. A week after our first session, the owner James had them walking on the lead OUTSIDE together. Something that would have seemed impossible a couple weeks ago.

Now I don't say this to toot my horn *"Oh Sean you're so amazing!"* No, I say this as any issue you're experiencing this book can solve as long as you're consistent, show your dog you're a calm leader and that you're committed to them. James was consistent from the moment I left that first session and he put the homework in needed to get to where he is with Butters and Blossom.

Remember that word I said I'd mention a lot in this book?

James was C.O.N.S.I.S.T.E.N.T with the training I had given him.

Now by reading this book it doesn't mean you will get quick results like James did, I hope you do, that's my mission and goal for this book. However, the thing is Rescue dogs just like other dogs have varied personality types and behavioral traits (I'll go through the behavioral traits and personality types in a later chapter) it's also breed dependent, so, for example, a Sheep dog's main role is to herd, it's in their DNA, that's their breed specific trait, but deep down to the core the role is to follow direction like all dogs so in their case it's from the Shepherd.

You then have. How long have they been in a kennel for? I have known a few I class as a "lifer" dog in rescue centers, that have been in there for 5+ years, so this is now the norm for them, but after a while even in a shorter time, problems can occur once re-homed.

You then have the history of that rescue dog: was he a stray? Was she beaten and abused? Was he used as a bait dog? Was she abandoned? The question of the problems can go on and on, but usually the more information you can gather when looking to re-home a dog the better, because then you have a better understanding of how to go about training that dog.

Let's imagine for a minute the dog you want to re-home was a stray dog before being rescued, abandoned and left to die, that dog roamed the street along with other stray dogs, finding food left from bins, generous people leaving out scraps or living of the wildlife. That dog was great with other dogs, he was calm around them, knew how to socialize, what he could and couldn't get away with, he knew his place in the pack and was a happy dog and rarely ever came into contact with a human.

Now that dog is in a rescue shelter, anxious and unsure. You know little about his history, as he was a stray. You take him back home with you; he backs off, needs his own space, possibly shows signs of low aggression (remember he's unsure of us humans) all he knows is how to be a dog and dog rules.

You try to get a collar on him and he runs and tries to hide. So, you do what most owners do; you treat him like a human. You let him upstairs in your bed, and on the sofa, and if you get him on the lead, he pulls like a train. He see's this as a sign of weak leadership, so he takes control and thinks he's the leader now. On walks he barks at strangers or other dogs, he jumps up; when you leave the house he whines, yelps and barks. You try to get him off the sofa and he goes to snap at you.

So what went wrong?

You treated him like a human, when he needed you to treat him like a dog, like the only way he knows and what dogs understand. They need leadership; they need a job; and that is to follow.

No, this isn't "old school" or "outdated" training methods, that most treat trainers and positive trainers would have you believe, hiding in these dog forums behind the computer screens. As soon as you put in the time to learn dog behaviors and why your dogs do what they do, these are the only effective methods that DOGS ACTUALY UNDERSTAND.

There's a saying "treat a dog like a human, and he'll treat you like a dog,"

There's more rescue centers now, who understand this

method and training. One I like to work with and will mention within this book is Just For Dogs and the work they do is great.

I always recommend finding a rescue center that won't just let you have any dog you want. *"Wow! Wait a minute Sean, how's that any good?"* this is good for a few reasons, the crucial one being a dog you like may not be the best match for you, your family, your lifestyle or what you want that dog for. It's in the best interest for you all if the rescue center workers help pick a dog for you, one that's best suited to YOU!

There's no point in having a retired Greyhound for example if your plan is to go on long hikes across the Peak District. There's no point in getting a reactive dog if you have another household dog. There's no point in getting a dominant bitch if you already have a dominant bitch in your house. There's definitely no point in getting a strong large breed if you are old or have shoulder or arm issues, as they're likely to cause serious injury if not trained correctly.

You get my point?

It's all about being open to the recommendations of the rescue shelter, and what they think would be the best match for your family, your lifestyle, etc. As at the end of the day as much as you might want to adopt a dog it's got to be the right fit for you both and personally I believe it's best not to have that dog in and out of homes because of the wrong choice of the owner.

An excellent rule of thumb for a reputable rescue shelter is when they ask you for as much information from you, the owner, as they can. So how many in your family? Do you have young or old kids? Other pets? What's your job? How many hours do you work? What's your lifestyle? Do you have a garden? Do you have any disabilities?

Then when the rescue shelter has accepted you and you've found your dog, they come and visit your home and check it is how you say it is, etc. Then usually in around two weeks get to know at what stage the dog is at; where you go in to the shelter, play with the dog and walk the dog, etc.

I know at face value this seems over the top. It isn't, it's always best to have the dog's interest at heart.

CHAPTER 3

THINK LIKE A DOG. NOT A HUMAN.

I know when I was I kid, I would pretend to be like an animal, I would crawl around with my older brother or even just pretend by myself, crawling through the grass, into my makeshift raggedy cardboard box den and pretend to be a dog. I would bark at birds, run around like a crazy animal, sniffing anything… well maybe not anything but to be a dog I had to think like a dog and it applies the same to when training your dog, well maybe not as extreme.

The following three points below are the key aspects it takes to tame a dog that has behavioural disorders;

1. Understanding the dog's psychology
2. Comprehending the dog's language (Behaviour)
3. Understanding how to calmly and consistently correct the dog and making a follow up through practical applications

DOGS THINK LIKE DOGS NOT HUMANS! It is important to understand that there is a sizeable difference between a dog and human beings. This is the first step to being a successful dog owner and trainer. Repeat:

1.   DOGS THINK LIKE DOGS, NOT HUMANS!

2.   DOGS THINK LIKE DOGS, NOT HUMANS!

3.   DOGS THINK LIKE DOGS, NOT HUMANS!

4.   DOGS THINK LIKE DOGS, NOT HUMANS!

5.   DOGS THINK LIKE DOGS, NOT HUMANS!

6.   DOGS THINK LIKE DOGS, NOT HUMANS!

7.   DOGS THINK LIKE DOGS, NOT HUMANS!

8.   DOGS THINK LIKE DOGS, NOT HUMANS!

9.   DOGS THINK LIKE DOGS, NOT HUMANS!

10. DOGS THINK LIKE DOGS, NOT HUMANS!

Ok I think that is enough of that, you get the picture, right?

I will go a little sciency brace yourself, it doesn't happen much.

Dogs are canines, so belonging in the Canidae family and then the sub-family of Canine. It is important to understand that the two **dogs and humans are different species**. This will help you understand that the psychology of dogs is different to that of human beings. Getting to know how dogs think will help you develop your dog to be as perfect as you wish it to be.

It is important to first understand that dogs are animals and they behave differently than humans. Dogs rely on their instincts to decide, be it responding to a command or anything else.

As you know, well I hope you do (some owners really don't), dogs are different when compared to human beings. For one, their choice of reaction to certain stimuli is is already written in their DNA. They can respond by fight or flight, so either fighting back, surrendering, eluding the danger or even running away from the situation.

These are the key core principles that are inbuilt and tell a dog how to respond in any situations they face. However, we as human beings have many options rather than the four which our doggie companions can make in such conditions.

So we humans beings are higher in mental capacity, well most of us are, that is we will handle a situation differently, we have much more tools at our disposal, so we might negotiate or barter, pretend to go along, manipulate the situation, get aggressive, try to be nice, the list goes on.

When a dog want's a bone from another dog they play fight for it, and that's it. You may get the odd dog that uses trickery. Now when we want something, we might fight for it, give up and let the other person have it, trick the person in to giving it us, walk away with it or just take ourselves completely out of that situation.

However, it doesn't stop there. We could also try to negotiate for ownership of the object through a court intervention, which then the court would decide who has the legal ownership of that object.

Wow, this object must be important now. Stay with me, give me a bone. Ah, I just said it. I'm getting to the point, albeit it a slow one.

Now the behaviour seen in our doggie companions tells us that their psychology, or should I say instinct, only gives them the four options above to react in. Now it's my job as the rescue dog whisperer, and this book, to work with the key principle that dogs can only obey us when they're ready to submit that leadership. So the goal is to get the dog to submit, show an acknowledgement of your leadership and this is accomplished by understanding that there is a sizeable difference between us as owners and our dogs.

As you know now, rescue dogs take correction and direction differently than we would. You should also realise that any bad behaviour from a dog usually starts from a single event in their life, so in most cases it begins from either dominance, insecurity, fearfulness or even frustration, and the dogs that cannot handle any of the above situations by just walking away or avoiding them usually steps it up to the next level which is dominance. Now a dominant dog is not fully the problem: there will always be a dominant dog. It's too much dominance, that's the issue, as it could lead the dog to become aggressive.

A Dog's Job

As we all know, as the saying goes,' it's better late than never,' but the best way to control unacceptable behaviour in your dog is right bang in their early stages… their youth or puppyhood: this is when it's happening. So, by now you know not to treat your dog like you would a child, as humans and canines are two different species and should be looked at differently. Dogs see the world differently: they aim to look at their human as their superior, their leader, so they should respect you.

I don't like to over-use the "pack of wolves" concept, as dogs are not wolves, far from it, but their basic instincts are the same. They still are pack animals and understand all the hierarchy that goes with it, so their behaviour is swayed by animal instinct, then dog instinct, and lastly their breed traits. They're calm animals by trait, and look to each other for direction, a job and a purpose, and they get that from their leader.

As you may have noticed both a child and a puppy can be quite the opposite of calm, well my children are anyway. So much energy, so much craziness. Atticus is a one child army ready to take me down, but he trusts and respect me as an adult, his Dad, and that's the same for dogs and this includes trusting people that are not deserving of that trust. But then a puppy will be hesitant to commands or before receiving direction, even at a young age they'll be monitoring you to see weaknesses within your leadership.

For a dog to trust or respect anyone, that person or dog must have earned it, they perceive love as an issue which will determine the whole fate of the pack, so if there's a calm and confident leader they must remain loyal to that leader... hopefully you.

A dog absolutely loves it when you give them a job or a direction, it makes them feel important and part of the pack. Unlike us humans that have ego's, (some bigger than others), which if someone corrects us, the big alarm bells in our egotistical mind go off and we get offended. Dogs don't get offended and take the correction as a direction from us.

A Dogs DNA

For the dog to become a balanced dog it needs to engage its doggie instinct, or its DNA. So, let's have a look at what all dogs share.

1. The need to be shown their job and to follow

2. The need to be given instructions

3. The need to be calm and to impose calmness

4. The need to work to benefit the pack

5. The need to be a balanced part of the pack

6. The need to take pride in brilliant work and be congratulated with affection from the leader of the pack

7. The need to make the pack survive harsh experiences

8. The need to coexist with the pack and be a major contributor of the pack

9. The three senses: Smell, Sound, and Touch and then also energy

10. The instinct to take charge themselves if there's no leadership

11. The instinct to protect whatever they think is part of the pack

Many dog owners believe in the misconception that dogs fulfil special tasks depending on their breed. So, for instance, some dog breeds are good at protecting homes, while some are bred for hunting, some are bred for pulling and some are the best for herding.

So, for example I know Jack Russell are breeds for ratting; they love to fit down those holes or chase rats that a ferret may have scared out. They are efficient and kill the rat quick, well most of the time, they might seem to love the activity for purely this, but the main drive is they are having fun taking direction and instruction from you, their leader, you've given them a job, a breed specific job but it's a job they love.

This gives them a sense of belonging as they feel like they are part and parcel of a team. This is also the same while you are playing fetch with your dog while at the park on that sunny day. It returns the play thing and waits eagerly for you to send it back. Think of it this way: directions and instructions to dogs, hugs, kisses and gifts are to human beings!

So, believe it or not when you see an owner madly shouting "Oi, Fido get here now, stop it!" they don't understand a word they're saying. Notice I didn't say "you" I know you're in the top 1% of owners, it's why you're reading this book right now.

Dog's won't understand what you're saying, but they will understand how you say it, so they will notice your tone. They notice if you're angry or sad and will take advantage of that and think less of you too.

This principle should guide you as a great dog owner:

1.   DOGS CAN'T PERCEIVE HUMAN LANGUAGE!

2.   DOGS CAN'T PERCEIVE HUMAN LANGUAGE!

3.   DOGS CAN'T PERCEIVE HUMAN LANGUAGE!

4.   DOGS CAN'T PERCEIVE HUMAN LANGUAGE!

5.   DOGS CAN'T PERCEIVE HUMAN LANGUAGE!

Repeat the above until it becomes your normal way of thinking. Well, I mean when you think about your dog, I don't want you to walk down the high street or at work shouting "DOGS CAN'T PERCEIEVE HUMAN LANGUAGE" I want you to finish this book at least before they lock you up in a madhouse.

Now it's understandable for most dog owners to not think this way, as it's not the norm we're told from other dog owners or passed down from generations. Also, as an owner, if someone else frequently gave me instruction and directions it would get annoying, I may have to throw some expletives their way.

Dogs, though, love to be follow directions and instructions by their leader as long as you're consistent and calm and follow through. Now, there can be more than one pack leader but if your dog respects you more than the other, when you're not around they may decide to not listen. The reason being they love you being around to give them direction as you're the more consistent leader.

Crazy time or calm time

So many people have the idea of letting a dog off lead to have a wonderful time and for their dog to burn off energy and go mental. The thing is this is where a lot of problems develop, especially as a puppy or a rescue dog where you haven't developed that leadership role enough.

Now a dog requires being calm and for you to be a calm leader so it can easily understand the commands you're giving it.

So, I'll share this story with you. It was a superb day, clear blue skies, sun was out but with a pleasant spring breeze, I was feeling confident from previous off-lead days with Lilla where she listened to my every command, so what did I do? I let her off the lead again, was practicing back and forth, sit and wait and some recall games, it was nearing the end of her fun time when she spotted a mum with her toddler in the distance; she looked at me, then back at the people in the distance and bolted towards them, not aggressively, but still at a pace. She excitedly knocked into the baby girl, knocking her over. It embarrassed me, franticly shouting Lilla to come back and then apologizing to the woman, who was fine with it all.

The thing I didn't think about before letting Lilla off-lead was that just 5 minutes before, a dog excitedly did laps around her on the park when she was on her lead... disrupting her calm. So, I let her off lead when she wasn't fully calm.

We live and learn.

Dogs are naturally calm animals, whether they're in a pack or at home eating. A calm dog should be able to focus, and can easily take direction and instruction from its owner, so going back to it, a calm dog can then contribute to the development of the pack - your pack. A calm dog should be able to resist the urge to hunt or chase when she sees a cat.

Now Lilla is temperamental with this, sometimes she's an angel dog, it's like she's not even noticed the cat, the next time it can be like tunnel vision and the only thing she sees is that cat. She'll pull, whine and moan as she wants to get to the cat.

A trainer who wants a dog to perform tricks, jump through hoops and run around obstacles needs to have their dog in a calm state to absorb the direction and instructions the trainer is giving it. A police dog handler who needs the dog to sniff out a certain drug needs their dog calm and focused to absorb the information the handler is giving to that dog, which is the scent in this case.

Now it's not fully the dog's responsibility, the owner,

trainer or handler need to maintain calmness in their dog by being calm themselves, keeping your dog calm should not be too difficult of a task, as dogs are naturally calm, I say this literally as Lilla is having a spot of zoomies around the garden. One minute I need to correct her and instill some calm!.....

Ok, I'm back! So, dogs, unlike humans, love and want to be part of a harmonious pack. They crave the idea of working together for the betterment of the pack and contributing to that common goal of having a strong, calm and consistent leader.

Now we for example can work together in a team but also by ourselves to achieve goals; we're more independent than our doggie counterparts. Dogs that are unable to behave according to their dog rules and have no consistent leadership will develop behavioral problems.

It is the understanding of most dog owners that dogs can understand our language, so when we tell them to sit, wait, down, for example, they follow through with their commands, but in fact they're only understanding those one-syllable words and the tone of how we say it. You could literally train your dog to sit by saying, "umpah lumpah" as they hear the sound and tone of how you say it! It would be outstanding if our dogs could talk to us and we to them.

I would ask Lilla why the hell does she really want to roll around in fox or badger poo or why she has the urge to smell that other dog poo. Yeah, I know very poo fixated questions. What would you ask your dog?

Acting on instinct or just ignoring you

As mentioned earlier in this book, the primary control of a dog's actions is its instincts.

Dogs wait for instructions from you, the pack leader, but if you cannot communicate effectively with the dog, they follow their instincts and act. So, for example, your dog might have acted badly in front of guests, jumping up, barking, whining etc. oh and we all know how they can cause the worst of embarrassments! So, you give it directions by correction, not direction by command.

The terrible thing here is that you are not the best dog rescue whisperer, most dog owners aren't. You shout at the dog, say NO! And give a few mixed command signals, which might confuse the dog more. The dog might stand still as it tries to digest what you are saying, as it naturally craves for directions and instructions from its pack leader.

So back to that story of Lilla charging towards that toddler and me shouting her name, commands and correction all at the same time. No wonder she didn't respond to me. What happens most of the time is that we as dog owners fail and the dog cannot understand.

The next thing you notice when your friends come around is your dog jumps up, his barking gets worse, he might display aggression to them and it continues to get worse as you continue to throw commands and corrections at random. The dog perceives you as a weak leader who cannot guide it, and so he takes matters into his own hands. He plays the role of the head of the pack until you get back to your normal senses, even if he doesn't have the personality trait needed he will still take charge and then he barks at the guests as guided by its instincts.

Dogs communicate through their senses, so senses such as smell, sound, sight, and energy around them and others, and then their body language is all defined through psychological qualifiers. The dog's psychological qualifiers are the same things that shape his behavior and leadership in a pack and how to be a dog. So as an owner your dog's perception of you is that you should master those psychological qualifiers for them to even consider you as a leader, so establish yourself as that calm and consistent leader.

So up to this point we have mentioned the dog psychology, the rescue dog's psychology and behavioral traits and the language they speak and understand. The next step is to develop a follow through system that is calm and consistent and with correction, see I mentioned consistent again.

All this should then be followed through by a practical action or command you want the dog to do. Dogs easily and best learn through calm, consistent follow-ups and being corrected persistently as and when needed.

Dogs have a job, humans have egos

Dogs are not human beings. It seems like I say this a lot, but I try to get away from the normal thinking of 95% of dog owners who humanise their dogs. Dogs act according to their base instincts and are eager to follow direction and instructions.

We humans, however, we're guided by social laws, along with our human instincts and then our individual reasoning. So, when dog owners try to communicate with their problem dog or let's say the rescue dog they have just re-homed, the communication will not be effective, and this affects the dog's behaviour; most of the time it develops unacceptable behaviour in that dog.

When we're corrected in any form, especially if it's repeated, we get annoyed. This is the opposite for your dog. When we correct a dog effectively to not jump up at guests, they take the correction as a means of direction, another job for your dog to take on board and please the leader. You.

They feel like they are being shown how they should behave when in your pack, and once a rescue dog can trust you, they feel the urge to fit in and be part of the pack and we rarely want to not follow the direction given by the leader. We need to correct the dog repeatedly for bad behavior and this is where the consistency part of it all comes in. After a while a dog might forget that inappropriate behavior or a learnt behavior from being consistently corrected and then praised for follow up of pleasant behavior.

If you remember that dogs are eager to please their leader and like to be told what to do next, (like going to fetch the ball, or to sit before crossing the road), the satisfaction they get is from the need to want to please their pack leader and that means being a contributing member of their pack. Ratting dogs or security dogs might seem to be overenthusiastic about their job, but they act that way because their pack leader told them to do so, and not following the direction of the pack leader is a sign of respect, that in the dogs mind could lead harm to the rest of the pack, remember that dogs want to work for the betterment of the pack.

Now the best dog owners are the ones that stay calm through the way they give their dogs commands, their body language and by being consistent. The thing is, most dog owners panic or shout instructions to their dog, using a correction like "no" and following through with loose commands. So here there is no consistency which confuses their dog, which puts them in the position, provoked by their instinct, to assume leadership, as they're now seeing inconsistencies in their leader's behaviour and body language.

As they wish the best for the pack, they assume that position of pack leader, which in most cases is when we have a dog behaving badly, but all its doing is assuming the position of alpha for the betterment of their pack.

Now you've picked this book up to start with maybe because you like the cover, then you read the blurb, you skim read the book and something stood out to you, or it has recommended it to you, but the main reason is because you're looking for solutions to your dog's problem and have accepted, maybe it's not just the dog, maybe you're not giving your dog the calm and consistent leader it's looking for.

Well, I'm here to say this book can help you and your dog. In the next chapter I will go into leadership in more depth, give you practical exercises, commands to use, why you need to ignore passive dominance... It's a juicy chapter, grab a coffee or tea and turn the page.

CHAPTER 4

YOU'RE THE LEADER - NOT YOUR DOG

Have you seen the movie animation "Up"? Me and Atticus watched it today for the first time, there's a part in it where theres a pack of dogs, well talking dogs that the old man and boy can understand because of a special collar. Anyway, the old man and boy get took back to their lair, and the pack is huge and guess who is their alpha... Drum roll, please. It's a human, a confident and calm old explorer. They do all their bidding for him and wait on his every command, even to the point of serving him and his guests dinner.

This is where it gets good. This is where you will learn everything 'dog'. The last chapter was really about why dogs do what they do. The mentality and philosophy of their doggie life.

This chapter will expand even more. As owners we need to understand that we are the leaders, we need to be the (It's corny) the ALPHA of our pack. If not, then our dog will take over, even if they don't have that personality to pull of being an alpha. So again, like I mentioned, that's where you get those behavioural issues you're experiencing right now, add this on to the fact you have just got a rescue or have had one a while and they have bought forward their past issues on top. You have a cocktail of disasters waiting to explode if you don't take control now.

The best thing though is, in this book, this chapter will show you the importance of positioning yourself as the leader, how to do it and how to show your dog you're that calm leader they need in their life. Remember, dogs are not natural leaders, their sole purpose is to follow that directive of the pack leader, it makes them happy; they love to please; they need that job, so when you give a command to your dog to sit, that's a job. When you tell your dog to wait at the door as you exit first, that's a job. When you get your dog to fetch a ball and bring it back to you, that's a job.

Now if your dog will listen to you it's a different story, because if he see's no reason to, and you're not displaying leadership qualities, then why would he?

As much as other uneducated trainers (yes, I will not beat around the bush) love to tell anyone they get in to contact with that 'alpha training is wrong, it's not science based, there's no such thing as an alpha leader in the dog world' but then shove treats down the dog to get them to do what they want it to do... Well guess what? That's getting your dog to respect the treat and not you.

The 3 major pack structures.

Alpha Dog–Mr or Mrs B.I.G the top gun, the one who rules the pack. The Alpha male and alpha female. The alpha, because they know they're the top dog, is not pushy or aggressive for no reason, other dogs will only challenge the alpha when it shows weakness or cannot provide safety for the whole of the pack. Other pack members look up to the alpha and look for guidance. Against what many people think, an alpha is not aggressive and will rarely fight. If needed he will be quick and to the point. They are very confident in themselves and their abilities and leadership role. When in a human pack, if you don't show you're the top dog and he or she thinks they're above you this is when you get bad behaviour.

The Beta Dog–Think Lilla my dog. So, she's dominant both passively and actively but has no clue how to be an alpha. When I was first training her with the behaviourist who trained me, she met another dominant dog, possibly an alpha, and they would get in to fights over mud patches and where they urinated, what toys were theirs, I realised it was Lilla who was constantly challenging the other dog - a confident husky which she briefly got the better of, safe to say they never met again after that.

Now the thing about that is a beta dog can easily be mistaken for an alpha dog in behaviour.

Now like I mentioned it's not the alpha dogs that are a problem, it's the Lilla's of the dog world, the beta dogs, who want to be an alpha but do not understand how to be one.

The beta dogs are hard to train, they're stubborn and really don't want to accept a lower position than they believe they should be, so will test you for the rest of their doggie lives. If you had an alpha and a beta together, they would always fight because of the beta constantly challenging the alpha. I like to think of beta as having a problem with authority and control. These are the dogs that most of the time are the ones that unfortunately get sent to rescue shelters as they're too hard for most owners to handle.

Omega dog–These timid dogs are mostly sweet and happy. They lack confidence and usually develop anxieties; they will try their best to stay out of trouble, but other dogs, mainly beta's, will sniff them out to dominate them. In the wild, omegas are usually bullied by the rest of the pack, usually for a wolf punching bag, but they also use it is also as an attempt to strengthen the omega, as the pack is only as strong as their weakest link. The anxieties with omega dog come if not socialised or acclimatised properly in their early years.

Pack Mentality

In the wild, all dogs even though they may look very different and all shapes and sizes and breeds, they still share that core DNA with their ancestors the Wolves. Now in the wild you have a pack, there's always an alpha male and female, and to most people's surprise the female is usually the dominant one.

The alpha gets first pick of the hunt and it goes down the line until you have the puppies or the omegas eating. The alpha is calm but when necessary will put other dogs in their place, this is usually in the form of air snap but can be a physical warning bite. The alpha will also sometimes side submit another dog if she feels necessary, this is where they roll and pin a dog on their back, this is a very submissive position.

The alpha will not be going up to other members of the pack for attention, she'll even ignore other pack members if they come to her for attention as it's on her terms when she wants to interact with other members of the pack. The alpha leads the hunt and the rest will follow, being an alpha you have to be a calm dog most of the time. But if the alpha shows weakness in her leadership, then that's when her leadership will be challenged.

The same applies to us as dog owners, even though you

might have a small chihuahua the same rules apply, in the dog world height doesn't matter, you could have a chihuahua and a great Dane, the funny thing is the chihuahua could be the one in charge as crazy as it sounds, believe me, I've seen a similar situation.

So how do you regain back control? How can you display those leadership qualities? The first place to start is the easiest but also the hardest. Makes no sense, I sometimes sound like the riddler from Batman, but let me explain.

Owners worst enemy... Passive Dominance

So what is passive dominance?

It's the minor things you are blindsided by that your dog does, and it's the things that you wouldn't have thought of as important before you read this book. Passive dominance comes when you're least expecting it, like that leaking pipe in the bathroom or the dog poop you stand in at the bottom of stairs first thing in the morning (yes that's happened to me) Your dog will not on purpose do these things when you're distracted, like for instance, when you're cooking, watching TV, playing with your kids, I could go on and on but I won't.

Here's what passive dominance is:

1.   Passing a dog toy and placing it on your lap or feet.

2. Rubbing their head or body against your legs.

3. Licking or nudging your hand for attention or fuss.

4. Rolling over on their back to tell you where to rub them

5. Rubbing their behind on you to tell you to fuss over them there.

6. Sitting on your feet.

Now your response to that probably was something similar to: "What! I can't fuss my dog or give them attention?" Now I sympathise with that, as the above just seems like normal behaviour.

Hell, before I learnt all this, I thought this was normal behaviour and if someone told me that, I would have been very sceptical too.

Now let me explain why all these are classed as passive dominance. Well now, with passive dominance (try to imagine in your head that there is a leader board), and on the left side is you, and on the right side is your dog.

All the passive dominance above are on YOUR dog's terms, they demand that you fuss them there or then AND in a certain place. So, have you ever had (now don't lie as all dog owners have), your dog come up to you, roll over on their back and then you've immediately gave them a big belly rub.

I'm guilty of that. So that's one point to your dog on the leadership board every time you do that.

Or, your dog comes up to you, places a ball on your lap or feet and wants you to play with them on their terms, without realising the reason why, you pick up that ball and you throw it away down the other end of the living room. So that's another point to your dog every time you do that.

You're cooking the best homemade lasagne, three types of cheese, it's smelling good. You're busy and distracted, your dog nudges his head against your hand or leg and you give him a pat or a fuss. That's one point to your dog on the leadership board.

Now, I guess you get the idea, and every time you let your dog do this. In their mind, that's one point to their leadership. Remember how I mentioned about an alpha and his pack? He'll only give attention to other members on his terms. What most likely happens to you then, when you go to call your dog over to get the ball off them, they back away, ignore you and make you follow and chase them. Yeah?

Now, how do we win this passive dominance game?

We act like the alpha; the leader!

Every time your dog comes up to you and does any of that behaviour: so if he passes a toy to you, if she licks your

48

hand, if he demands a belly rub, if she sits on your feet. YOU IGNORE THAT BEHAVIOUR. That's one point to you on the leadership board and every time you do it you rebalance the scales. So now you're on top.

Easy as that! Well, as long as you pay attention, even when you're most distracted.

Consistency is the Bone (Key)

Ok, you've heard it before already and guess what? You'll be hearing it again, much more.

Anytime you think about being a leader the first thought that should pop into your mind is "I'm a calm CONSISTENT leader of my pack" Your dog needs that consistency, that routine, you telling him which directive to obey and follow. Remember, it's his job, he wants to follow you, he happily wants to do what you tell him to do, he wants to show you his loyalty.

Here is one of the greatest dog stories ever told:

"Never mind, said Hachiko each day.

Here I wait for my friend who's late.

I will stay, just to walk beside you for

One more day."

- Jess C. Scott –

This was the story of Hachiko, a Japanese Akita dog, who's incredible loyalty for his owner, Hidesaburo Ueno, who continued to wait for over nine years following his owner's death.

It makes you think what sort of owner Hidesaburo was. I can imagine he followed the principles I outline in this book: calm and consistent leadership with correction and follow through. You're only as good as you're consistent. All this training is nothing if you're not consistent with the training that I give in this book.

I hope you get this point as I mentioned consistent/ consistency 5 times, oh wait that's another one, 6 times I mentioned it, and I did so because of how important it is.

The leader leads

In the dog world the leader leads, where the alpha goes the

rest follows. That translation in to the human world means, if we walk with intention the dog must follow behind if we want them to BUT it also means that we don't follow them, we're the leader remember.

So the way this works and how you practice this rule is when you walk through doorways, YOU walk through FIRST. Easier said than done, as what usually happens is your dogs try to beat you to it, or rushes past you to get through first. Therefore I recommend closing doors when first practicing this, don't worry they get it quickly.

So say you go to a door, if your dog is being stubborn and doesn't follow, call him over. Now tell your dog to wait, slowly open that door, if he tries to get up correct him (Don't worry I mention the correction in a later chapter) then tell him to wait again. Your goal is to open that door fully and your dog is waiting and then for you to walk through first and then your dog follows behind you.

Practicing this will show a change in the dogs perception of who you are; you're now showing signs of a leader to them. Your dog might come up and sniff you to check if you still are who you say you are. Really this happens a lot. It's like they think "Oh wow something's changed here, this is not my owner… think I need to smell him now to make sure"

Height is dominance

In the dog world, height is dominance. You may notice it when dogs fight. They try to get height over the other dog, but it doesn't always mean being physically higher than their opponent. In the human world, and as a dog owner, the height is dominance rule, is when a dog is on the sofa or a bed: it raises their status in their head. Also, when you pick them up again, that's a sign to them you're saying they're the leader. I will mention you're allowed to pick a dog up, but it HAS to be like a baby, so the dog is on its back, in the cradle position.

I know these rules sound bat crazy! To us humans anyway, but this is not humans we're talking about, these are dogs, they think completely differently to us and have different social constructs to what we have.

It's why we have to enforce these rules. So, you would not allow your dog on the sofas for 2 weeks, then after 2 weeks it's invitation only. Ideally, also not allowed upstairs, but if you do, then don't let them on the bed. I'm sorry if you don't like that one. I know the feeling; I used to spoon two Jack Russell dogs when I was a teenager. Don't make the mistakes I made. Remember, height is dominance. You will not be doing yourself any favours, and most definitely not your dog.

Dominant behaviour, warning signs

Now I always recommend for you to correct any dominant behaviour. A confident, dominant dog can get out of hand quickly if you let them get away with and display these behaviours. It can also stem from insecurity, this then leads to frustration, that then leads to a low form of dominance, which if unchecked, goes onto a higher form of dominance, like aggression:

1. Putting paws on humans or dogs

2. Laying or leaning heavily on you or another human or dog

3. Showing signs of anxiety towards another dog

4. Toy or food dominance

5. Growling or barking at humans or dogs

6. Assuming 'prey pounce' position

7. Correct a dog if it's too close to what you think another dominant dog is

8. Face-to-face meetings with another dog

9. Mounting dogs or humans

10. Neck or ankle biting in dogs or humans

11. Mock biting you when being corrected

12. Focusing too much on an object obsessively

So, you must correct any of these behaviours. Don't worry, we will get to the correction part soon.

Dominant and Submissive body language

So, dogs are experts at body language, especially with reading us mere humans, but as an owner you need to know the body language signs to look out for. This one alone could save you a lot of heartache and hassle.

Signs of dominance

- Tall and erect

- Ears upright

- Head high

Signs of Submission

- Head lowered

- Tail lowered down, in between their legs

- Ears moved back flat

- Licking lips (can also mean aggression or anxiety)

So, these are the things to look out for, but what you need to be aware of is your dog is continually watching you for signs of weakness in your leadership, so that's body language. They'll know when you're not happy, when you're stressed, playful, sad, and they'll definitely know when you will not follow through with the correction or training. They see this as a sign of weakness.

Your body language needs to be both calm and assertive. You need to keep your height when correcting or giving commands, so don't bend down to their level when correcting them.

Leader or Follower?

So how does your dog see you: Leader or Follower? It might be a surprise to you, you're probably following. try to answer these questions.

1. Does you dog try to walk in front, not looking back at you? This can be inside and outside of the house. Does she tug or bite at the leash?

2. When she is playing does she bring you the toy? Bark at you? Or play show and run?

3. When your dog want's attention, does she:

   A). Sit on your feet?

   B). Barks or makes noises (whining included)?

   C). Rest head on any part of your body?

   D). Stares at you?

4. When going through a door, does she try to beat you through the door?

5. Rarely responds or pays attention to you when you want her to?

6. May jump on the sofa, chair or bed uninvited?

7. Does she lean her body into you or sit/lie on your feet?

8. She growls or doesn't move when you try to budge them off the sofa or take a toy away from them?

If you or anyone else has been snapped at, bitten or attacked by your dog (my advice is) get in a dog behaviourist to sort out the behavioural issue before trying any of these trainings tips and exercises.

Quick cheat sheet

Now, because I'm nice to you, I'll drop some early practical training advice in, but you must read the rest of the book to get the fuller picture. Here is what you need to do:

1. Teach him sit

You need to teach him "sit" first before asking for it. If you have great, you're a leader, if not, let's get to it. Every dog needs a leader, if you do not take the position he will. Dogs will be placed in to this position either by choice or no other way. All family members need to do this, (adults or kids over 12).

Remember, a leader is always calm, and cannot meet aggressiveness with aggressiveness, so I recommend not trying an alpha rolls or neck shakes (FYI an Alpha roll is where you roll your dog over on its side until it's calm, it's a way some dog behaviourists used to assert their pack dominance).

Use your height so stand up straight and using the correction "AH" sound to let him know you mean business. In the next chapter, we will get to learn how to correct properly.

Your dog needs to know nothing in life is free. So, when I say this, it means your dog must earn everything he gets. Sit is what he needs for anything he wants. Dinner? Sit (only say it once) then correct. Keep at it until you get him to sit, if you give up remember that leader board, that's one point to him.

You control all the marvellous stuff: anything the dog want's or likes. If he wants to sleep on the sofa, get him to sit and wait and then invitation only. This is how a leader acts, and it may be tough thinking you're protecting your rescue dog, but this is exactly what they need, a calm and consistent leader.

2. No pulling – walk to heel.

Do not let him pull you on a walk, do not let him lead the way; in his mind he is leading you to hunt and forage. A good tip is to let him toilet before you set off on your walk, as then it won't be a panic to toilet straight away on your walk and he shouldn't want to pull as much. The goal is a loose lead walk, so that would be at the side of you, not pulling where his head is no further than your longest stride or even where your foot falls. He also doesn't get the benefit to toilet when he wants. If he tries to, carry on walking: it's a strict walk on your terms until you get to the area you decide, maybe the park or a patch of grass, then he can sniff, toilet, roll around or lie down, it's his time, fun time. When he's walking well, praise him lots.

Now if he tries to lead in the house, like trying to beat you to doorways or second guess which direction you're going in, then you can block him in his tracks with your body or sometimes it's better to change direction and not go in the way he wants or trying to herd you to (herding breeds do this) you might have to do this for a while, you may get dizzy but you need to get him used to not trying to beat you and wait for you.

3. Ignore, ignore, ignore.

Remember when I said you ignore passive dominance? Ok, so when your dog comes up and places a toy on your lap. IGNORE. If she barks at you, correct. After she gives up and walks away, then grab that toy and make it the most exciting thing and call her over. Now it's on your terms, but just as exciting for your dog.

If she tries demand your attention, so rubbing her body against you, pawing at you, nudging your hand with her head, you also ignore this. If she barks at you when you're ignoring her, that's when you correct that behaviour, as barking is unacceptable.

4. No Jumping

Do not allow your dog to jump. This is behaviour that needs correcting. Do not encourage jumping in any form. This is where you get to the tough point.

If you've been practicing this point before, you'll know of the stranger danger. Your walking with your dog, you see someone approaching you with a smile on their face; they make doggie noises to your dog, your dog gets excited and jumps up, pulling you forward, and the stranger than gives your dog a big fuss, before you even get a chance to tell him you're training your dog not to jump up.

5. The Wait command

So, this is a great command to come after "sit" or just even on its own. For example, when your dog is about to rush through the doorway you could correct with "Ah" then use the command "Wait". Say it like you mean it. What will most likely happen the first time is your dog will ignore you. This is where a leash comes in handy, so you can gain back control and check your dog as he's on the lead. So, say, "Wait" if you're feeling confident, or you could say "sit" and then "wait" then YOU go through the doorway first.

6. Look at me

You might not have as much success with this when they are puppies or adolescents. So, start by saying, "Look at me" and hold your hand towards your eye like you're doing an 'ok' hand sign. When your dog looks at, you give big vocal praise and a pat on the head.

7. Don't sleep with your dog

I heard you gasp for a moment. You might nod your head in disagreement right now… Well, who cares. We as owners, as leaders, don't sleep with our dogs. I used to religiously every night for the best part of 3 years. I was in my early twenties, and let my two Jack Russell's sleep in the bed with me, sometimes spooning them… yeah, let's forget that ever happened.

Dogs don't get this privilege to sleep in the best places, where the leader sleeps; it gives our dogs the wrong signals. Now they can sleep in their bed or crate next to your bed - but not on or in YOUR bed.

8. Don't pick your dog up, unless like a baby.

Remember, height is dominance. You may have been picking up your dog in the usual way (usually small dog owners). We have the tendency to carry them around everywhere we go, well please don't, trust me, it will help you long term. If you really want to pick your dog up, then do it like a baby, so on their back, which is a submissive position. Also, don't let them sit on your lap, if you do, the same thing applies; you can then have them on their back on your lap.

9. No Biting please

Has your dog bit you before?. Ok...this one involves creating scenarios, so your dog can't get into these situations where he's bit you. So, no pleasant treats like a tripe stick or pig's ears until you're confident he can then drop the treat when you say so. Also, no sofa time for your dog. Now this might mean closing doors or not letting them in certain areas of your house until you know this is better or have gotten a behaviourist in to help you resolve those issues. It's always best to get a vet exam to be sure nothing is medically wrong to cause aggressive behaviour.

Some dogs will get worse before they get better, sometimes much worse, which is why I advise getting in a behaviourist to help you and your dog. Obviously, this book is here to help with that, but for more personal one-to-one training I also offer online training. For those who are not local to me go to:

www.onedogtraining.co.uk/online-training/

So you now know all the basic quick tools to adopt to become the leader. In the next chapter I will show you the correct way to "Correct" your dog, and no, it's not what 95% of dog owners do. Read the next chapter to become that 5%

CHAPTER 5

CORRECT LIKE AN ALPHA, NOT AN OMEGA

I was a right shit as a kid (excuse my French) in school; I was all about the showing off, which was strange as I was also mega shy. I didn't like authority and when a teacher told me something, let's say correct to keep things relevant to this book, I would protest and I was determined to do the opposite. It's probably why I got put into isolation a lot. Well, the thing is when a teacher talked to me on my level, on a level I could understand… guess what? I listened, and I did what they told me too, and this is what I will teach you to do with your dog. Talk to them in a way they understand.

So now you've gone over some quick steps in the previous chapter and can move forward with gaining back leadership in your pack and to show your rescue dog that you can be the leader that they need right now. The next step that this chapter will cover is correction, and no, it will not be "NO" like around 95% of owners use, and that just doesn't cut it for the other 5% of dog owners out here looking to be the leader of their pack and resolve any behavioural issues like you want to resolve.

The correction I teach and that you will use to 'talk dog' and get them responding much quicker to you will show you the results and respect you want as the leader. Now the correction is basically what the mother would have used to correct her pups. I remember seeing a video that perfectly showed this. It was a room full of puppies, maybe ten of them all going crazy biting, fighting and chewing things in that room, oblivious to anything going on around them. Well, a minute into the video the owner let the mum into that room, she calmly entered and gave off three low sharp growls, for the ones that didn't listen, it was just a couple of growls again, and all those puppies stopped what they were doing and lay down looking like a naughty toddler that had just been told off.

If I hadn't known what I know now about the correction and why dogs do what they do, I would be shocked and amazed. This way of correcting is exactly what I will show you, and used in the right situations, calmly and confidently, can have the same effect. I will teach you to 'talk dog' as corny and overused as that sounds, but the fact is that's exactly what I'm teaching you.

So when using this correction, you need to keep your height. Remember height is dominance, and for the correction to be effective we need you to use your height. Now I don't mean you have to be tall like me, no, I just mean to stand up straight and look taller than if you was slouching or kneeling down at their level.

'AH' your way to success

Most dog owners correct dogs with the English language. Funnily enough, the dog stands still or is frightened and runs away; you would think they understand what is being said. However, for you to correct a dog effectively, establish yourself as the leader of the pack, and be able to speak its language. This will ensure effective communication with the dog. So, the correction from now on I want you to use is "AH". Yeah, just that, but I want you to add a growl, with a back of the throat sound to it. So "AH" but with a growl. Now this can be a little more difficult for females to do, as it requires the huskier sounds we need, but I've also seen some of my female clients correct a lot better than me, so it all really depends, just don't use this as an excuse. Repetition and practice are key.

There are also Four stages to the correction, or should I say progressions: these are like little add ons you can do to bring attention to your vice more, so they are:

1. Correction and clap AT THE SAME TIME. So, this means as you go to use the vocal correction "Ah" you also clap with your hands at the same time.

2. Correction and shaker bottle AT THE SAME TIME. So, you vocal correct and then shake a bottle with stones in at the same time as you correct.

3. Correction and water bottle AT THE SAME TIME. So, as you vocal correct, you use a water bottle and spray your dog from the neck downwards at the same time as you correct your dog.

4. Touch Correction – So this includes using a vocal correction along with a quick but light finger poke to the side of your dog's legs. DO NOT use this touch correction on aggressive dogs, you can't fight aggression with this form of correction.

Now that's the hierarchy in the order you would use them, if the one above had a minor effect ramp it up a level and go on to the next progression. The reason for the above progression is it helps to bring extra attention to your vocal correction "AH" and reinforces that correction. Now don't get into the habit of using the progression but not saying the correction. It's the correction that has the most powerful effect, not the extra part to it. So when your dog is barking you don't just want to use the water and not say the correction, you need to vocal correct "AH" and squirt water at the same time.

Remember this and you'll succeed

To a dog your voice, or should I say tone, is important. This is what they will respond to, and the training commands you use. Usually when a dog stops listening it's because you, the owner, are not using the right tone or you're not saying the correction like you mean it. If you stick to the points below for the use of correction, then you will not go far wrong.

- **At all times** use your correction like you mean it. Don't half-heartedly say it as your dog will know if you mean it or not and this will be the big decider if they listen or not. Say it like you mean it to save a lot of future headaches… trust me I know, when starting out I did the exact same thing, I'm telling you not to.

- **At all times,** after correcting, use the right command for the desired action you want your dog to do. So, if you would use "down" to tell your dog to get off something, then the next time don't say "off" so pick your command and stick to it.

- I recommend "sit" for sitting, "Down" for lying down. "Off" for getting off something. "Wait" to get the dog to be still temporarily, and "stay" to get your dog to stay for a longer time.

- **At all times** after every correction follow that through with a vocal praise, but only when your dog stops doing the unacceptable behaviour that you want him to stop doing. Also, notice how I said 'vocal praise' and not 'physical praise'? If you go down to physically praise your dog after something good it negates the correction. A pat on the head will be enough at this stage.

- **Never** use physical force to stop your dog's destructive behaviour. You can't fight aggression with aggression or scare your dog into listening. Now, there are forms of physical correction as noted above, but I do not see these as aggression.

- **Never** use your dog's name as a correction or negatively. For example, I would never shout "Lilla down!" to stop her from jumping up. Only use their names positively. The bonus of practicing this is it will help with recall when you get to that, as they respond to their name as you've been using it positively.

When correcting your dog's behaviour timing is key. Anticipative correction is where it's at. If you can expect unacceptable behaviour before it even happens, then you're on to a winner.

So once a poor behaviour has happened, so say for example your dog has barked at a cat walking by the front of your house, you then have 5 seconds to correct that behaviour: ideally you would correct him at that exact time. The reason being is if you correct the behaviour after that time your dog will not have any clue why you're 'talking dog' to him. So it happens within the first 5 seconds of it happening, then followed by vocal praise if he's stopped doing what you wanted him to stop doing.

Now I don't want to be the bearer of dire news, and no I'm not a psychic, but at some point your dog will stop listening to you again, and you'll be like: 'this training isn't working'. Realise that it's not the training or your dog... It's you. It's the reason you picked up this book, right? You knew you needed to learn more and be that leader. When this happens and it will, it's because you've stopped saying the correction correctly.

So instead of "Ah" you've said "Urhhh", instead of saying the correction like you mean it, you've said it half-heartedly, instead of correcting when you use the water bottle, you've noticed every time you pick up the water bottle your dog stops that behaviour so you think you need not use the vocal correction.

If you fall into these unwelcome habits your dog will fall back into their unwelcome habits, which may be continuously barking for no reason/ reactivity on the lead/ aggression/ separation anxiety/ pulling on the lead: the list

SEAN PURDY

goes on. Whenever you notice this happening, check back to this chapter.

The rescue dog correction

Now you have a rescue dog and you might remember me mentioning about how when corrected they might go in on themselves and retreat, become scared or become aggressive. You then have to use your own judgement on what correction progressions to use, with the more anxious dog, a quiet vocal correction may work better and come across less aggressive, whereas with a more confident, dominant dog that has been used to being in charge, a correction lead with the vocal correction and shaker bottle might be the best option.

The rule of thumb here is that it's always best to start at the beginning; at the lowest form of correction. So that would be quite a mellow vocal correction "AH" and then judge from there if you need to ramp up the correction to the next stage and so on.

What you don't want to do is use a higher correction straight away on an anxious rescue dog that may have has previously been abused by humans, as that dog will then go the opposite way and may not trust you again or find it hard to build that trust back up.

Again with rescue dogs, get as much information from the

rescue centre as you can from their previous lives. The more you know, the more you'll be able to adapt a training routine for them. Now I understand that the rescue centers can only tell you what they know, but with this there are also some rescue centers with better practices than others, ones that have the dogs' interest first. It's sad to say, but this happens, and I want you to know this so you can understand, and do your due diligence, if you haven't yet got a rescue dog, or if you plan to adopt more.

Hopefully, you now understand the full use of the correction and how to use it, and when things go south with the training to first resort back to this chapter, and then Chapter 3 also, to get your leadership and correction to where it should be. In the next chapter it's time to get practical: time to get hands on with training. I will give you exercises to practice with your dog to nail down this leadership in the house, get your dog walking to heel when on a walk, to get their attention on you with attentive exercises, then slowly introduce you to recall exercises on a lunge lead. All this working to establish you as a calm and confident leader.

Don't worry, you will also learn some fun games to play with your dog in your house or garden. And when the weather's not great, and you're not feeling like a lengthy walk, but your dog still needs to burn off some of that energy and boredom.

CHAPTER 6

TIME TO GET PRACTICAL

With a rescue dog, many things can affect their training. It could be their personality trait, previous training they've had or not had their experiences with humans, such as previous owners or other dogs, or if they were stray dogs plus more to boot. So I believe when training a rescue dog, to begin with, is its fun for you too! don't worry it's fun for you too.

In my training I like it to be fun, because a dog always learns quicker this way, but they always still need that leadership, and like the previous chapter a great correction; the correction I teach in this book.

So the nice and easy exercises I like to start with that are pressure free are scent games, sniffing - and a dog having to use its smell sense is a big deal for dogs - it's just something we seem to forget about at times. It triggers a dopamine release (the happy hormone), and has been shown to increase confidence and reduce anxiety in dogs (so even better for the anxious rescue dog!) so, essentially, it's a natural stress reliever. It's also very much pressure free, so your dog can take part at their own leisure. Remember, it's FUN.

When I first tried these with Lilla, she was hesitant. She was like: "Wait a minute! What are you up to?" but soon, she realised it was a fun game where she got rewarded, both in treats (food) and lots of vocal praise.

These are a quick, easy and fun way to bond effortlessly with your rescue dog, that is nonaggressive and can be in a safe and calm manner that your dog will understand.

Do these exercises first, to test where your rescue dog is at. Ask yourself:

Does my rescue fully trust me yet?

Does my rescue respect me yet?

Are they food driven or praise driven?

Ok, so if you answered yes to the above questions it's up to you if you want to practice these fun rescue dog starter games, I would still recommend that you do.

Hide & Treat

So grab some treats, ideally raw treats. I did just say raw, but we'll go on to that in a later chapter.

1. Pick your treats

2. Walk around your house or garden and start hiding treats, don't let your dog see where you are hiding them all.

3. Once you have finished hide another one in plain site and then say the command "Go Find"

Magic Cups

1. Grab those treats again.

2. Get three plastic cups.

3. Hide one treat under one of those 3 cups. Let your dog see.

4. Mix those cups around like you're performing a magic trick.

5. Then say command "Go find"

Right so these two will help you break the ice with your non-trusting, "who the heck are you hooman!?" rescue dog. They'll help create a stronger bond, and like mentioned above, are non-aggressive, so will help with trust.

Where to start...

The recap before training starts

Dogs need a calm and confident pack leader to decide every decision for them, no matter how lame it seems, that's what they like. For example, moving forward or backwards, left or right, how to enter and exit doorways, walking to heel at the side, behind you when walking through doorways. Dogs were born to follow; they were not born to be leaders over their inconsistent owners. A dog's job is to follow a directive or job given to them by their owner, they want to know what their job is and in knowing this they then feel like they've become a contributing member of the pack. So, a dog's absolute number one job is to follow you, the pack leader, a dog needs calm, direction and protection. Their job is to be a contributing member of the pack.

I don't enjoy repeating myself because I like the sound of my voice, or mental voice as I'm typing this, but I believe repetition and consistency is key and the more you hear and practice something, the more that thought will be ingrained in your mind and will become a habit.

The 3 rules to follow

1. **Consistent giving of direction and correction–** so remember in the last chapter how I said you have

around 5 seconds to correct your dog's behavior, after that your dog most likely will not understand why you're correcting him.

2. **Immediate correction and expecting the correction** – So expecting the correction is correcting the behavior before it even happens, immediate correction is to correct as the dog is doing that behavior, so in the moment correction. Now expecting a correction is the ideal way: it's better than immediate as you correct that behavior just before it happens so the dog doesn't even get the chance to misbehave. Now trying to do this all the time will be impossible, so don't stress when you can't do it.

3. **Always finish what you start** – If you correct a dog and then give it a command; even if that command takes 10 minutes for your dog to perform, then you wait 10 minutes. When first training Lilla, I made the mistake of trying to get her to sit before crossing the road; she put her foot down and was determined not to; it took over 20 minutes of me going back and forth until she gave in (Yes, I was determined).

Let's build the foundations

These will be the building blocks on which your rescue dog learns the rules of the pack; establishing yourself as the leader and showing your dog you're a calm and consistent leader. Up to this point I will presume you've read all the other chapters before this one, and that you understand the use of the correction "Ah". Now it's time to program that correction into your dog so your dog understands the context coming from you. He'll notice a change and think, "Wow! Wait how does she know how to speak dog!" throughout the programming stage he might even come up to you and give you a sniff to see if you are still the person he knows. Ideally there will be two of you to practice, one to correct, the other to get the dog to misbehave. If you are by yourself, do all the process yourself.

No Jumping up

In my world jumping up is not allowed, it's not even acceptable from a small dog, because in their head they're dominating you. If you've rescued a large breed puppy, it may seem cute and small at the moment, but give it 8 plus months it will be a lot bigger and jumping up won't be fun anymore.

So, for jumping up you will get as exciting as you can, bend down slightly, pat your legs and make excited noises. If you notice your dog thinking of jumping up, the other person will then correct "Ah" and continue to do so maybe every 2 seconds. So vocal correction "Ah" then count in your head 1, 2 then vocal corrections "Ah" and repeat until your dog has 4 paws on the floor.

You want to repeat this until your dog second-guesses trying to jump up at you. What usually happens is they sit down and look at you. If your dog doesn't respond to just your vocal correction (Yes, some dogs are stubborn or dominant) that's where the next progression comes in... remember the correction progressions I mentioned in Chapter 5?

That's where the vocal correction with a clap of your hands at the same time comes in; this will bring more attention to your vocal correction. So here you make your dog jump up, then you or the other person corrects and claps so you're following the process above, but you're adding in a clap. You notice that 95% of the time your dog will listen, but if they don't, then follow the next progression.

Jumping on Furniture

Now I briefly went over this in previous chapters, so I won't go over the reason again why you should not allow your dog to jump up on sofas or beds uninvited.

Ok so the below part you can use this to program in that correction, so making sure your dog knows that correction, so, for example, if your dog does not want to jump up at you, Sit on the sofa like you usually would and I want you to invite your dog up. When your dog jumps up, I want you to stand up and vocal correct your dog "Ah" and say command

"Off" then repeat the process until your dog does not jump on the sofa. You should follow a no sofa rule for two weeks and then after that invitation only. You should not let your dog go or sleep on the bed, I know you might hate me for this, I'll get a bad rep etc. etc. etc. Well I don't care, don't let your dog on the bed unless you don't want behavioral problems to be resolved...or like you like to wake up to your dogs bit's on your face.

Answering the door for you.

So, this is one where you will have to set the scenario up, because if you wait for someone to come to the door to practice this, you will be under prepared and you will not expect it. Have someone go outside to the front door while the other stays inside with the dog ready to correct. The person outside then knocks on the door or rings the doorbell and you go to answer the door, but your dog has to be ten foot away from the door.

We don't want them answering, you may have to correct a few times, tell them to wait and stay, and then go to answer the door. If your dog gets up, walk towards them and correct "ah" and use the command "wait".

Repeat this process until your dog is calm and then let your guest in. Your dog HAS to be calm when greeting the guest, not jumping up or overly excited. Tell your 'guest' aka your partner/friend to ignore for the first minute and then to call your dog over and give praise.

Pretending not to hear you when you call their name

Ok, so believe it or not, this is common… and it's a lack of respect. So, remember in previous chapters how I said I want you, when calling your dog's name, only use it positively: so you would never correct your dog and use their name. The reason being is this: when you call your dog's name you want the association to be a positive one, so they don't pretend to ignore you and they come to you when called, this is especially important when out at the park. Don't worry; I've got some games to come later to help practice this one a lot.

Now you can use a lead in the house. You bend down excitedly, call your dog over, if they do not respond, you stand tall again and vocal correct, then bend down again and excitedly call them over. Repeat and rinse. When your dog comes to you, praise her.

You go through doorways first

Don't let your dog Usain Bolt through the door before you; this even includes the front, or backdoor, always gets them to wait. Ideally, you start with doors closed for easy practice of this. So, what you want to do is get up and head to a doorway, if this is a problem issue with your dog what will most likely happen is, they will bolt straight out the door before you. Now before that even happens you need to vocal correct "Ah" and say command "wait" you may have to use your leg to block your dog. Close the door. Slowly go to open the door, correct if you see any sign of movement, remember the aim is to anticipate bad behavior and correct it before it happens, keep blocking with your leg and open the door fully, correct once more and give command "wait" then you walk through the doorway first, tap your leg and say "This way".

When exiting out of your door when going on a walk, you will most likely have a lead on, so you can vocal correct and then say "wait" and hold back with the lead as you open the door and then exit first.

Naughty biting or mouthing... Big NO NO!

Any form of biting is a no, no. Remember, you're the pack leader, do not let this happen. This usually happens with a dominant dog or one who gets into an over excitable state. This is where the bigger progression comes in to play more, whenever your dog bites or tries to mouth you, you vocal correct at the same time as squirting water on to your dog from the neck downwards (those mayonnaise bottles are great for this) or if you have a half check lead you correct him on that (will explain later) always remember to be calm and firm.

A dominant dog will mock bite its owners arms and hands

in a show of leadership. The best way to correct this is expecting the bad behavior and correcting even before that excitable state of mind happens.

Food guarding aggressiveness

So this is where you go up to your dog's bowl and they turn around and look at you, and look like the devil dog, teeth all snarling, eyes in the red zone.

So how to resolve this?

Leash lead your dog. You MUST be CALM as you're practicing this exercise, any tension in the room will not help this situation as your dog will already be on the edge as she knows something is about to happen around her food bowl. So, walk up to the food bowl while your dog is on the leash, and wait in front of the bowl until your dog looks away, sits or even lies down, let's say for 2 minutes. You want this to happen before you even think about feeding your dog.

Now if your dog tries to move away, leash correct her away from the bowl, you might have to block her path either with your body or a mop or a tennis racket. You do this until your dog gets the picture and loses interest.

Once your dog is calm for those 2 minutes, slowly move your dog in the food's direction and let her eat it. While this is happening, you do not mess or pick up the food bowl. Once your dog has finished her food take away the bowl, you can hold the lead out away from you when you do this or get someone else to remove the food bowl, your dog must not react when you're doing this, if she does, correct that behavior.

Resource Guarding

With this one, I always recommend that the owner leash the dog and wear shoes to be on the safe side. You will claim all dog toys by stepping onto them and then correcting your dog both vocally "Ah" and chain correction on the half check collar. (A chain correction is basically where you tug on your lead, which they slightly pull on the chain part of the collar, making a chain noise)

Your aim is to keep correcting bad behavior until the dog is in her natural state of calm and loses interest in the toys, so they may move away or sit and lie down near the toys.

Once the dog is fully calm, you can then use one of those toys to call your dog over to play. Remember, with play: you start the play and you finish the play.

A Frustrated dog

With any signs of frustration in a dog you will vocal correct "Ah" and if you need to use correction progressions, I

taught you in the previous chapter. What to look out for in
frustrated body language:

- Licking movements of the tongue, usually when
  anxious as well.

- Rapid eye movements

- Fixation of a person, object or another animal

- A hunched over stance, low body and again fixated on
  one thing.

- What I like to call crazy eyes (You'll know when you
  see it)

- Pacing About or obsessive behavior that only happens
  when a dog doesn't know how to respond to a situation.

Toilet problems

Rescue dogs can and will toilet in the house in the first few
weeks, mainly because of a change of territory, uncertainty,
unfamiliar people and smells. Without rules in place a dog
will toilet out of the assumption they are the pack leader
and they can toilet where they want... crazy, right? Other
reasons are:

- No set feeding time

- Leaving food bowl out all day.

- Not watching for signs of needing the toilet, so twirling around, sniffing at the ground, waiting near the back door or whining and begging at you.

A way to resolve this issue is first follow what I've been saying in this book, assume pack leadership and be consistent. Second go back to puppy training. So, keep to these six reference times to let your dog out to toilet:

1. First thing in the morning.

2. Before bed

3. After a nap

4. After a play

5. After food

6. After water

If you let your dog out after these times and assume pack leadership, you're covering all areas and your dog should stop toileting in the house quickly.

Leash Leading

This is not as confusing as it sounds, and I'm not saying for your dog to lead you. Here's what you do: put a lead on your dog and let it drag loosely with the dog, you do this only under supervision and for the first couple of weeks, but you do this as it quickly allows you to get control of your dog for correction, so if your dog jumps on the sofa but is not listening to you, when you're telling him 'down', you now have the lead on him, and you can vocally correct him and also lead correct him.

Using a muzzle

It's always an excellent idea to have a muzzle when you think it's necessary, especially with rescue dogs when you know a brief history about your dog you're adopting. It helps you, the owner, feel safe and go through with the training, and if you're calm, then the dog is calm.

I say this because I remember when I first learned how to become a behaviorist; I had a client with a big German Shepherd with aggressive tendencies to humans. Instead of going straight to using a muzzle which would have made my life so much easier and the training a lot smoother, I carried on without a muzzle, even when first answering the door, and Bert lunged towards me, snarling and teeth out, all warning signs telling me to watch out.

For two sessions I carried on teaching the owners to train Bert. I was fully hands off. To be honest, the training was going well but could have been faster. I came to my senses on the third session and it all pieced together. My energy and Bert's owner's energy was much calmer from me doing this.

So my lesson to you… NEVER second-guess using a muzzle.

You can use muzzles for socialization training with other dogs and humans if you know your dog has had a dog on dog or dog on human aggression previously. Also, always use a muzzle when first socializing your dog with a child; don't be that kind of owner.

Then ONLY remove the muzzle when training is 100% in these situations and you have full trust and respect for your dog. Safety always comes first, and I don't just mean it for you or other people or dogs, I mean this for your rescue dog. He could attack the wrong dog, and that could be the end of that story.

Great Segway to my next part…

Child Training

No, I'm not telling you to train your child, if you have one. Well, Atticus could do with some training now and then, even though he loves to copy Daddy and correct Lilla.

When any children are present, muzzle and Leash lead your rescue doggie. You always want your dog calm when around children, now I know you may be one of those dog owners who haven't got kids or even hate children and are muttering all expletives under your voice because I'm mentioning children in my book read this part, you never know when you might need it.

Just a quick tangent, I remember seeing a Facebook post where one woman, we'll call her Jacky, was asking for advice as she just gave birth and she had not long adopted a rescue dog, (Reminds me of my origin dog story) anyway, she asked for help and then in the comments one woman went off the rails berating this woman "How dare you mention children on a dog group, I hate children Blah! Blah! Blah!" Anyway, I'm sure you can imagine how that went for her. Anyway, the moral of this story is, don't be like Jacky.

Anyway, back to the training. Correct any behavior when around children, this includes:

- Over excitability

- Dominance

- Aggression

- Anxiety or insecurity

- Basically, any behavior that is not calm

Remember the story where I mentioned Lilla running up to that toddler and bowling them over? She was over excited, and this should have never happened.

So calm is law around children. Do not allow your dog to herd, wrestle, mouth or jump on children. Be calm with your dog until you're confident you can trust your dog around children.

Separation Anxiety

Go about as normal as you would before leaving the house. The same routine, for example get your coat on, grab your shoes, jangle your car keys. If your dog paces or whine or get nervous, correct that behaviour. You can only leave when your dog is calm. So again, go towards your door, get your dog to sit and wait 10 feet away from the door, decide on an invisible barrier they're not allowed to pass. Your goal is to get out the door without the dog whining.

Before that, any time your dog whines correct that behaviour, get them back ten foot and start the process again. If you get out the house and your dog whines and scratches at the door straight away, go back inside and correct and repeat until there is no reaction.

Once you leave your house the first time, what will most likely happen is your dog will moan, whine, yelp, run to the sofa or chair and try to look out the window.

When you practice this training, practice this in 5 minute increments so 5, 10, 15, 20, 25, 30 etc but the first time let's stick with two minutes. After two minutes of no whining or reaction you can then enter.

Do not fuss or praise the dog for the first few minutes, an alpha ignores the other pack when they demand it, only when the alpha decides.

Dog Crate Anxiety

So when you put your dog in the crate, and they play hell and whine and yelp like you're torturing them... then this is for you.

Put your dog in the crate like you usually would, close the door and start to leave the room, if your dog is calm. If your dog is not calm, then correct the dog until they're calm and then start to exit the room again. If your dog whines and moan again, go back in and vocal correct that behaviour, sometimes you may need to use water. Correct until your dog is calm again and repeat this process.

You should follow increments of 5 minutes, but the first being two minutes, so 2, 5, 10, 15, 20 , 25 etc and so on until your dog does not whine or react to being left in the crate. Remember that the aim is to let your dog know that their purpose and job is to not react and whine when left in the crate alone without the pack.

Fearfulness and Insecurities

A fearful or insecure dog needs to face their fears head on and calmly.

I will use Lilla as an example here. There was a stage when Atty, in his crazy toddler state, chased Lilla in his toy car. She had her Lead on and it somehow got wrapped around the toy car which frightened her and she charged in the house with the toy car trailing at the back of her, I quickly reacted and Lilla and Atticus were fine. Well now, every time Atticus went on his car Lilla freaked out. She huddled close up to me and hid. This is a big no, as we as the leader do not want to feed that dog's insecurity.

So, what do you do?

You need to let them know they need not fear this thing. So, with the Lilla Cargate situation for example, I had Lilla on lead in proximity to Atty and his car. Every time she reacted I corrected that behaviour.

Insecurity and fear are behaviours that needs to be corrected, not fed. This is a lot better for the dog's health. So, I kept correcting until calm happened within Lilla and every time she reacted I corrected. Then I moved a little closer and repeated the process until she stopped reacting to the car.

This is how you help your dog get over fear and insecurities, not by mollycoddling them.

You're probably thinking "Wow Lilla is a real problem dog" Yes she was, she's hard work, well still is but it's consistentcy she needs.

Excitement and anxieties

Correct any time your dog shows over excitability or anxiousness. These include jumping up on you or other dogs, pawing you, other people or dogs. Basically, any behaviour that leads to excitable or anxious actions.

Remember your dogs natural state is CALM, when a dog is not calm, they are off the natural balance. Now I'm not saying your dog can't be excitable, they can, but it's in certain situations where you can't allow, as a leader, for your dog to display over excitability. The story of Lilla bowling over that toddler is one of those situations.

Walking to heel

Ok, so before leaving for a walk everything should be calm, that's including you. If you're feeling stressed or anxious, don't even bother as it will be a crappy walk, and will put you in the wrong mindset for the next walk. You want easy wins for yourself and your dog so you can progress quicker. So, the walk begins before even leaving the house.

You're in the house and about to go for a walk. You get your dog on the lead, get them to sit, make sure they are calm, and stand at the side of them and walk a half circle around to their other side. All the time you're doing this your dog should not move from their spot. If they do correct them, tell them to sit and then wait. Once you get to their other side, walk back to where you started and give them their release command. Something like "Ok" or "Ok then" or "Free" and directing them forward with the lead.

Repeat this a couple of times, and once you have a few success's before even leaving the house, you've set the tone for the walk.

Before setting off on your walk to make sure your half check collar is the right fit, you want to be able to just fit two fingers under it as it's tightened on your dog's neck. Note: the half check NEVER chokes your dog, it's used to train your dog through the noise of the half chain and the slight tension of the collar tightening.

Go to the front door, your dog must sit and wait, so tell them to sit and then wait. As you're opening the door your dog's bum must be planted on the floor and you must walk out the door before your dog. None of this dog rushing past you, omega owner type crap.

The goal of the walk is for your dog to walk at the side of you, pick a side and stick with it, no pulling, no looking around or sniffing; this part of the walk is on your terms.

Ideally you will walk your dog on a halti 6ft lead and a half check collar (Check next chapter) any time your dog's shoulder passes your knee or the full stride of your foot, you correct with the check of the collar.

The check of the collar is you pulling, like a flick of your wrist on the lead, so the half chain on the collar makes the checking noise and tightens to the width of your dog's neck but never chokes your dog.

Every time your dog looks, or moves left, you check them the opposite direction. When they pull forward, you check them back. When they slack behind you check them forward.

You catch my drift?

This requires patience. But here's the excellent thing, if you don't have as much success with this, say your dog is being stubborn, I have a couple of attentiveness exercises for you to use.

Awareness #1

I base these exercises on getting your dog to pay more attention to you when on a walk and so on a lead. Start by walking your dog to heel (on the left of you) when your dog goes in front of you, turn in the opposite direction, so always turning away from your dog, as you turn and your dog does not follow, check and say the correction and then say "This way". Praise your dog when they follow.

The command "this way" is important, as by using this repeatedly when on lead, when you let your dog off lead, using the command " his way", your dog should follow you.

Awareness #2

Start by walking to heel and again, and as soon as your dog goes in front, take a step back at the same time as dropping the lead from your right, while still holding on your left, slight check on lead and correction and then turn in the opposite direction.

Awareness #3

Start by walking to heel and when your dog walks in front of you take a few steps back whilst checking and correcting at the same time once your dog is back in line walk forward once more.

These entire awareness exercises compound on each other, so start with the first and use Number 2 and 3 when needed.

Once your dog is walking well, you go to an area, so if there's a patch of grass, or on the park, that's where they have their time, to sniff, toilet, roll around, etc. This is usually the time you can swap leads and attach to a lunge lead, which I'll go over in a moment.

Dog on dog Reactivity when walking

With any poor behaviour when walking, it's best to first

muzzle your dog and to expect it, so remember anticipative correction and get it before it occurs. Obviously this is easier said then done... I know.

The best route of option is to keep correcting and walking forward until you have passed the thing your dog is reacting towards. Also remember to always be the barrier between your dog and the thing they're reacting to. So, if you were walking your dog and your dog was reacting to another dog across the road, your dog would be farthest away from the road.

Also, when your dog is reacting to a dog across the road, you can stop and let your dog watch (the other dog) and keep correcting your dog's inappropriate behaviour, then turn and carry on walking.

When meeting new dogs with reactive dogs it should most definitely be 'bum greetings' so your dogs nose to the other dogs bum or the other way around, if you have a friend who has a dog, go on a walk with them, their dog in front and you walking 5 or 10 metres behind them to begin with.

Every time your dog reacts keep correcting until calm, then move a little closer, keep repeating each time until your dog is calm, You want to get to where you can get your dog to sniff the other dog's bum, 95% of the time when your dog does this, he'll feel a lot calmer with this dog. Keep setting up situations like this and before you know it, that bad reactivity your dog had will be close to non existent... As long as you're consistent.

Dog on human reactivity during walks

So follow just like above with the correction when your dog is reacting towards another person, so you can carry on walking and correcting or you can stop still and correct as your dog is watching them walk by. If you want to practice this, you can use the technique where you get friends or family over to muzzle your dog to be on the safe side, and have your dog on a lead at all times. When your dog reacts towards that person, you correct that behaviour until calm happens within your dog.

Remember, consistency is key here, it might not work wonders straight away, but it will work. You're telling your dog, as the leader, that this person is not a threat to them or the pack, you're in charge, and this is unacceptable behaviour, your dog's job is to follow your commands.

Walking multiple dogs at the same time

The same thing applies with multiple dogs as it does with one. You get them to walk on the same side; they sort out where they place themselves, usually the more dominant one will be on the outside. When any of them pull, you lead correct, this will only correct the dog that is pulling on the lead not the other dogs, as their leads will be slack.

The reason that you don't walk your dogs on either side is that it places you in the middle as the subordinate; you're a leader not a subordinate omega. Once coming back to the house, remember you must enter the house first, so get your dog to sit and wait. Again, you must be able to open the door fully and you go in first before your dog gets up and comes in.

Long-lead training

So I use a 10ft horse lunge lead from decathlon, great material but nice and cheap. Perfect for long lead and recall training. Also, for safe socializing, and for easy access for correction. Let's assume all owners are not as knowledgeable as us. They let their dog of any temperament off lead and do what they like. It's your job to spot the dominant and excitable ones, these are the dogs that tend to correct other dogs, which as you can an imagine could lead to fights. Look out for:

- Those crazy dogs that sprint super quick past your dog (Kind of like Lilla on her crazy days)

- Dogs mounting other dogs

- Dominant dogs

- Dogs meeting face to face

- Dogs pawing or jumping at other dogs

So, it's your job as pack leader to expect these dogs behaviors and correct the behavior before it happens. This is sometimes tricky.

Whilst on the lunge lead, now and then call back your dog, use correction and then command, "come". When you use the command, bend down and sound exciting, like you would when you talk to a baby.

Long lead awareness #1

Always get your dog to sit and then wait when you change over from a walking lead to the lunge lead. Once they're swapped, you can give your dog the free command and let them have their time for a couple of minutes, so they can sniff, toilet, and roll around. Once you're ready, walk in the opposite direction from your dog, always watching your dog the whole time, then when your dog comes up at the side of you, turn again in the opposite direction. Keep repeating this for five minutes, or until your dog is turning when you do and is following you.

Long Lead awareness #2

When on the lunge recall lead, similar to awareness #1, you want your dog to keep guessing, so when your dog catches up at the side of you turn in any direction, like you're zig zagging, always turn away from your dog though, not in to your dog. If your dog does not turn, lead correct and vocal correct and say command "this way". Keep practicing this until your dog is turning with you.

Long lead recall #1

Still on the recall lunge lead, if your dog is getting to the full extent of the lead or they've tried to run up to another dog or person, gently tug on the lead and say command "this way" and you walk away from them, whilst keeping an eye on them. If your dog ignores you, you correct and tug on the lead again and say "this way". You gently tug on lead and say correction at the same time and repeat the command "this way".

Long lead recall #2

When your dog gets to the end of the lead (if you're practicing this first couple of times use half of the lead) say their name, (this is where being positive around their name now comes in hand) call them over and say command "come" and gently tug on the lead. If they ignore you repeat the correction and command, if they come to you, praise them as they're walking up to you, if at any point they veer off, stop praising them and correct them and say "come".

Get your dog to come to your side, get them to sit and wait and then use their release word, so something like "Ok' Or

"Ok Then" or "Go on then" which then teaches them they can go away as they've done what you wanted them to.

CHAPTER 7

BIG QUESTION... WHAT EQUIPMENT??

The right equipment matters, right? It's what helped me run a marathon in 2014, I'll explain. I used to do just what I see everyone else do, buy those clunky Nike trainers with that big ole chunky padding at the bottom because that's what they tell you help, when in reality for me it did the opposite.

It wasn't until I researched I fell in love with Vibram 5 fingers, running shoes that fit around your toes and creates the feeling of barefoot running. What's barefoot running? It goes of the past that as cavemen, we would of not had trainers and most likely ran barefoot, feet used to this with its natural padding, its great and needs a fresh approach to running, plus if you believe in this, it centers you to the Earth. Well, I ran hundreds of miles, possibly thousands in those trainers and never looked back because I found the right equipment to do the job.

Why equipment talk then? Well, I use some equipment a

lot of trainers or owners don't use, and I mention these in the book. What kind of dog trainer would I be if I left out this section to leave you guessing... A crappy one is what I would be.

Well, luckily, I'm not. This means though if you have not got the equipment, you'll have to grab some spare change and get the equipment I recommend. Which, as you've saved a ton of money by buying at a fraction of the cost of my one-to-one training, these will be a brilliant addition to your training.

Halti 6ft training lead

This is a great sturdy lead. I feel confident when walking Lilla and my clients have said the same. The best thing I like about it is you only need this lead. It's interchangeable as it has 3 separate rings so you can either walk on the 6 ft lead, then you can shorten it by a third and then again by half. My partner Tania uses it on the half setting whereas I use it as the full length.

Half check collar

This is the must have equipment in my form of training. It's a grand piece of equipment. Now it comes off the back of the choke collars but this is a half check; it doesn't choke your dog in any shape or form. You tighten the collar around the dog's neck so you can just fit two fingers under the chain when at full extension, so any time your dog pulls, it only tightens to the width of your dogs' neck. The brilliant thing about this is it trains your dog by the sound of the chain noise, every time you lead correct and also by tension again by the lead correction.

10m Horse lunge-lead

You've probably read this thinking: "why the hell would I need a horse lunge lead?" it's made of great material, well made, and won't give you rope burn, well especially if you have a big dog who might have the tendency to pull suddenly. These are great for practicing recall, as you have the safety of the 10m lead, and as far as your dog knows they're off lead having fun all at the same time and you can get them under control or practice recall.

Please note, these may be overkill for the smaller breed dogs. You could always attach two 6ft leads together.

That's it! These are the only things you will have to really have to fork out for. Well, apart from a mayonnaise bottle, preferably the Hellman's variety.

Water bottle – So once you have used up a bottle of mayonnaise or BBQ sauce, clean it thoroughly and fill with water. You'll notice if you tip it upside down the water won't come out unless squeezed. Great!

So you will use this as described in previous chapters as a next step up on the correction ladder.

Stone bottle – So just like above, this one is simple DIY. Just fill a bottle up with stones or even rice and you will use this as a noise correction to go along with your vocal correction. It helps break your dog out of barking or jumping up as it helps bring attention to your vocal correction.

Not essential for all dogs, but still great to have:

Halti – So you've most likely used or know of someone who has used a halti in your dog owning life. My partner will sometimes use a halti when walking Lilla. I think it's mainly because in the past, when she was an untrained dog, she broke Tania's finger, but sometimes she has her good and bad days, so Tania will put a halti on as an extra precaution.

The halti works by controlling your dog's head movements; they say when you control the head you can control the direction and stop them pulling. You might notice your dog runs for the hills… metaphorically , it would be more for the sofa or somewhere to hide, once they realise the halti controls them.

CHAPTER 8

FUN GAMES AND TRICKS TO TIRE AND ENTERTAIN

I'm a 30-year-old man but can play like a child with the best of them, I'm just a big kid. I played with figures until I was 15 years old, yeah I know slightly sad but what I'm trying to get at is games are fun, for us and for our dogs, your dog will love them. It helps bring that bond between you and your dog much closer, especially with a rescue dog who needs more time to adapt and trust you.

The Games and tricks

Snufflemats

Lets make a snuffle mat, you may wonder "what the heck is a snuffle mat Sean?" They're mats that allow your dog to find dry food or even treats that you've hidden in the big mess of entangled fabric. It's a superb way to make your dog's food last longer, but also a magnificent way to stimulate their brain as they try to sniff out the food you've hidden. (Obviously not suitable for raw food).

Now you can buy these online. Just type in "Snuffle mats" and you'll be greeted with numerous ones to buy or you can make them yourself. The super duper easy way I know of is to grab a pile of old unused material, old clothes, socks, towels and just thread and tie them together, use the ones online as inspiration, get creative and at the end of it you'll have a fun sniffing mat that your dog will go crazy for, plus it keeps them busy.

Now I made one, well I should say Tania made one, I don't want to be sleeping in the doggie bed tonight. She used one of those old milk man plastic thingy me bobs to carry the milk in; you know? Well, I hope you know.

She tied some old fabric around that and then all I do is throw and mix around some treats and Voila, a home-made diy snuffle mat, that Lilla goes bonkers for. Check my YouTube channel out for the video of her seeing it for the first time.

The Finger flip treat

Ok, very simple but fun, once you master it... Well should I say your dog masters it too. Place a treat on your thumb, so imaging how you would with a coin when you go to play heads or tails, well this is exactly the same thing but with a treat.

Get your dog to sit, show your dog the treat and then place the treat on your thumb. If the dog is looking at you, say "Ready" and then flick the treat so it goes above your dog's nose, the aim is then for your dog to catch it in their mouth.

I've mastered about a 90% success rate with Lilla, depending on how hungry or distracted she is.

The Master Kong

Everyone Knows of a kong, or should know of a kong. It's that great big, apparently indestructible poo shaped rubber toy, the one you fill with your dog's favourite food. I mean proper stuff the food in there and then shove it in the freezer. Once frozen you give it to your dog and Voila, it should entertain them for a good 30 minutes.

Now you can get kongs in many sizes, the size I use for Lilla is the XL black version, but their standard version is the smallish red one.

Now a great free alternative to a kong, but it won't last as long, is to give them an empty peanut butter tub (xylitol free peanut butter) Lilla literally sticks her tongue right in there, usually distracts her a good 15-20 minutes.

Bang! Play dead

This one is fun to learn and is a gigantic step up from the previous games and tricks. Your dog should already know commands "sit", "wait" and "down" before you practice this. I managed to teach this Lilla in around 2 hours total over 2 days.

Grab your dog's favourite treats, get your dog to sit and then lie down, once they have lied down, you want to lure them into the play dead position on their side. Grab the treat and hover near their nose, then move the treat over their nose and to the side to get your dog to roll over onto their side, say "Good" and then give the treat. Repeat this step until your dog is doing this effortlessly.

Time to add the signal, once your dog can do the above get it lying down then use a hand signal with a vocal cue, so in this case a gun hand signal and say "BANG" then with your gun hand do the same motion that you did with the treat to get your dog to roll over. Repeat this.

Once your dog has got that, practice this in the sit position and then finally practice with your dog standing up.

Frisbee and ball

Find out which your dog likes the best, play with them each and encourage play using your best highest pitch fun dog voice, praising them. Then just stop and hold on to that toy until your dog releases. Repeat. Then give your dog their second favourite high value toy, play with it like above while holding on to it for a minute or two, then release and let them play with it for 10 seconds.

Now get their main high value toy out, again your highest pitch fun dog voice, be as exciting as you can, get them to drop that toy and give them the one you have but not fully; still hold on to this one and when you've decided it's the end, stop moving, as you get your dog to release it using command "Leave it"

Now this game is significant for:

1. Establishing what your dogs favourite toy is.

2. Teaching a "leave it" command.

3. Making yourself more interesting than how they currently think you are.

Eye contact

Well, not exactly a game but can a quick training time and as a distraction. Get your dog to sit, say their name and then command "Look". When they look to give lots of vocal praise, every other time give them a treat. Do this for 5 minutes, multiple times a day.

Your dog's superpower... Sniffing!

I'm a comic geek; I love superhero movies and now I've slowly noticed Atticus loves them too.... I'm trying to limit the t.v watching. Well, I love the X-Men especially the

Wolverine character: a husky, can't die, looks middle age man but over 100 years old mutant. There's a part in the movie where he looks up into the air and sniffs, trying to catch a scent. Well, this is when Atticus said "Daddy doggy!"

Well this is a doggy's main super power that they all share. 30% of a dog's brain is dedicated to analysing smell. That's 40 times the area of the human brain. The dog's nose contains around 300 million olfactory receptors compared to that which we have, which is a meagre 6 million.

There's an outstanding example in Alexandre Horowitz book *Inside a Dog:*

"We might notice if our coffee's been sweetened with a teaspoon of sugar; a dog can detect a teaspoon of sugar diluted in a million gallons of water: two Olympic-sized pools full."

To me this is a dogs super power that's not to be sniffed at…

So it makes sense to make games around just this. Playing some nose games with your dog teaches them this is a good old fun time with the leader and it's on your terms.

I remember watching an episode of Rugrats, you know, where they're talking babies and toddlers. Well, they have a dog called Spike and in one episode I remember the dog had smell'o'vision it was all different colour and it was an added ability that helped the dog make sense of his environment. He also heard people to him talk like "blu Bla Bla bu buro ba ba!" which is a slight tangent going back a few chapters where dogs don't exactly understand human language, but tone.

Anyway, to not use scent games with your dog is like clipping birds wings and caging them. So, lets get to it.

Command "Go find"

This is a brilliant way to bond with your dog and get your dog practicing their smell sense. Now you might think "My dog couldn't smell a sausage if it was in front of his face" trust me, I thought the same of Lilla but she soon got the hand of it. Just think of it as a much slower version of find and retrieve. This works especially well if you have something your dog REALLY wants.

Remember how I told you about their favourite toys? Well, you can do the same process with your dog's treats (food).

Basically, what you want to do is show your dog the thing they want, make sure your dog sniffs it, then get them on the lead as you hide that thing, make it obvious to begin with like slightly under the sofa or behind a chair. Once your dog finds it, give them lots of vocal praise. Repeat this for another four or five times.

Next time you hide it, put it somewhere else. What you don't want to do is make it too difficult for your dog straight away. Get those small wins in early and then progress, based on your dog's abilities.

Hide, Treat Seek

Grab a small handful of treats, show them your dog so they can have a good sniff, then go hide them treats around your house or garden; remember not too hard to begin with. When you have done this say command "Go find" your dog will then hurriedly rush around the house or garden, nose to ground sniffing all the treats out. Now only practice this once a day. You don't want a chunky overweight dog.

An easier and simplified version of this is basically going to your garden or on a field (on a lead) and scattering some treat on the grass, then getting your dog to sniff them all out.

Go find daddy… or mummy

Now instead of a treat or toy, you go hide. Ideally, you play this game with two people. One of you holds the dog as the other goes away and hides, remember to make it easier to begin with, then once you're in the other room, the other person releases the dog, say command "Go find daddy" once your dog finds you, praise like crazy.

What I like to do when on a walk in the forest with Tania is to go hide behind a tree. I have Lilla's ball; I let her see me go behind that tree, Tania is holding Lilla at this point, then she either turns Lilla around or covers her sight and I go hide somewhere else. Then Tania releases Lilla and again says "Go find daddy" what usually happens is Lilla goes to run up to that tree, her smell sense kicks in halfway, like she's thinking "Oh wait a minute, they've done a switcharooney!" then she uses her smell sense instead of her sight and she finds me.

At this point me, Tania and Atticus go absolutely mental when praising and Lilla loves every minute.

Dinner time

Any chance I get to practice scent games, I do it. So now when I feed her, her dinner...(I feed raw, so two chicken carcass's) I have hidden them in the garden, then I go get Lilla and say the command "Go find" her ears prick up and she excitedly scurries off, nose to the ground, sniffing out her dinner.

Obviously, if you feed kibble or wet dog food, this might be a little more difficult to do, but you could do this with pieces of apple, raw dog treats or some scraps off your plate; just an excuse to play more scent games.

CHAPTER 9

HOW FAR CAN YOU TAKE YOUR TRAINING

Ok, you've got to the end of this book; you've gained a lot of knowledge, straight out of my head. Thank you for getting this far and reading my book.

What to do now?

Well, you can head over to amazon and leave me a great review (well if you think this was worth it) tell everyone what you gained from it, the best parts, how it's changed yours and your dog's life, and then share with all your doggie owner friends.

What's next for you?

Well, dog training is not a one hit wonder, as you now know it takes consistency and with some dogs if you drop the ball in your training, they will try to take control, so now it's up to you to stay consistent, keep a daily training routine up and be that calm leader I know you are.

I've given a lot of my training, as much as I can cram into this book and taken all the fluff out, but there's only so much a book can give, sometimes a one-to-one is needed.

There are plenty more things you can gain from a one-to-one session:

- One to one, hands-on training

- Practical walkthrough of training exercises

- Lead training

- Recall work with toys

- Off lead training in paddock or safe area

- Aggression training

- Adventure walks, training

- Scent training

- Dietary advice

- Mentoring

So if you want it, the option is there, I also have a ton of free content on my website and my Facebook group "Derbyshire Rescue Dog Training Family" where I'm regularly adding fresh new content.

Yes, it's free.

See, it's not just enough for me you read this book, I want you to succeed and have that well-trained dog.

The thing is, you need to take action and be consistent.

I always say 80% of people who read my content, be it free or paid, including this book, won't take action or do anything about the training I give.

The fear of change or perceived hard work will put them off.

Then you have 20% who will adopt maybe some training I give: they have sporadic success, their dog still tests them and is generally confused, yeah, they might have stopped jumping up or barking but the behavioral problems are still there.

Then you have the 5%, the owners who take it all in, who adopt 100% of the training I give and have transformed both themselves and their dogs' lives through the dog training steps I give in this book. They understand dog behaviors and why dogs do what they do.

The excellent thing about this is, you're the one who decides where you want to be in those three categories.

Do you want to be the best owner and that super calm and confident leader your dog wants?

Well, head over to www.onedogtraining.co.uk and book a one-to-one session with me to take the next step on your dog-training journey, I can train at your home (Derbyshire area) or I offer online sessions, plus keep an eye out for my online courses coming soon. Alternatively, go to the free stuff tab under resources.

My Free Gift To You

Why a free gift… or two, or three? I want to help you even more, to be able to take your training that you know now and easily be able to apply it for you and your dog and to see some hands on training.

You've taken the dedication to pick up this book from thousands of other in a bookstore or let's be honest amazon and have it in your hands when you could've picked another book.

You have decided now is the right time to help yourself and your rescue dog out (This book helps out every dog too) So I admire that. I want this book to be one of those books that you can continue you look out and chip in and out of, not the ones where you read once and then they collect dust on the book shelve.

I hope it achieves this and now I want you to put what you've read into action from reading Rescue Dog To Super Dog.

Solving all your dogs behavioral issues should be top priority to you and implementing all the advice I have given in this book should be applied, trust me I know they work, I have used every single one of them in my life with Lilla and my clients dogs.

1. **Gift number 1** is the free digital version of this book that you can have easy access to on your phone or tablet, for those times when you just want to dive in to the book quickly on a certain topic. Go to

    www.onedogtraining.co.uk/resources/free-stuff

2. **Gift number 2** is an hour-long client call regarding my leadership training 101, you can be a fly on the wall and see how my sessions work whilst also learning all the useful leadership training, basically the foundation to your training. In this video I have a client regarding separation anxiety, we go over all the foundational exercises and rules and also some walking to heel advice. You don't want to miss this. Go to

    www.onedogtraining.co.uk/resources/free-stuff.

3. **Gift number 3** is the power point presentation from the above video you can take time to analyze and apply the principles; this is a great add-on to the book. Go to

    http://www.onedogtraining.co.uk/resources/free-stuff

ACKNOWLEDGEMENTS

Rescue Dog To Super Dog is my first book but not my last.

If you've been part of my community, you'll know a hell of a lot about me by now, my business my highs and lows, trust me I've had both but a lot more highs that's for sure.

You'll know Lilla as the ever-testing dominant beta bitch, who's had every problem under the sun, bar separation anxiety, but without her I wouldn't be here now, writing this book and talking to you.

I'm also where I am because of my die hard "never give up" attitude. I continuously keep on trying and getting better and I try to surround myself with that company.

You should to; you need to find your own doggie community with the same like-minded approach and principle to training.

I have an outstanding team in my life. I wouldn't be here without them. These are the people, the reason that I do what I do and the people that have pushed me or inspired me.

Obviously my family comes first.

Tania, my beautiful soul mate, without her, her hard work in looking after the children when I've been out dog training, or finding peaceful moments to write my book, she has been there with me through all of it. Her hard work ethic and success in her career has driven me further with mine. Then there are my children, Atticus and Aurelia, who I'm lucky to have and inspire me to be and do better.

Mum and Dad who did an outstanding job in bringing me up, my Mum who has always supported my endeavors in life and who proof- read this book for me. Thank you.

Darren Purdy - My brother who brilliantly designed and illustrated the super Lilla character on the front of the book cover. Thank you.

My mother-in-law Sue, for giving me business advice and continuously supporting the family. Thank you. - www. hathayogawithsue.co.uk

Margaret Smith from Just for Dogs, without her and this significant rescue center in Ashbourne, Derbyshire, I would have not found Lilla. She has also spurred me on without realizing it to be the rescue dog whisperer and to write this book. Thank you. – www.justfordogsrescue.co.uk

Dom Hodgson – The pet business guru who has helped

and inspired me to expand my business in so many ways and to help so much more people. Thank you. - www. growyourpetbusinessfast.com

My **Derbyshire Rescue Dog Training Family** Facebook group. You inspire me to be better and to help you out as much as possible. Thanks for supporting me on this journey.

Finally, to every one of my clients, thanks for believing in me, thanks for listening to me, thanks for singing my praises and recommending me. Without you, one dog training would not exist.

ABOUT THE AUTHOR

Sean Purdy is straight to the point dog behaviorist, with his no fluff no BS, very effective and fun style earning him his status – "The Rescue Dog Whisperer". Sean is the leading solo rescue dog behavioral expert training owners to easily understand their dogs for results that will last a lifetime.

Owner and creator of one dog training Sean has helped many a dog owner and their dogs, be it rescue or puppy through the hard times and behavioural issues to then give the owner the tools and skills needed to help their dog understand their place in the pack and the confidence to look up to a calm and confident leader in their owner.

To find out more about the training services, coaching, courses and book go to https://onedogtraining.co.uk

To enquire about booking Sean to speak at an event, podcast, radio interview or anything else email to enquiries@onedogtraining.co.uk

Sean lives in a beautiful village with his fiancee Tania, and his two children Atticus and Aurelia and their dog Lilla.

One Last Thing

So you've finished my book completely, hopefully this is not the end and you can chip in and out of this book when you need to. What I ask of you now is if you found help out of rescue dog to super dog then head over to amazon and leave me a positive review, it helps more people like yourself with a rescue dog needing help, and let's me know I did a great job and that I continue to provide quality books.

Keep a lookout in this space, plenty more books to come.

Until next time.

Sean Purdy

Printed in Great Britain
by Amazon